Testimonials about Ron Hequet and his Business Growth Strategies

"Ron, I learned what I know from you! That led to Fruit of the Loom hiring us to manage their inventory and the formation of IDEA, L.L.C. Boom! I'm rich and it's all because of you! My hero; thanks, Ron. You are the greatest!"
Henry F. Camp, CEO, Louisville, KY

"Ron, I really appreciate what you've done to turn my business around...to lead me on a path of success and profit! Thanks...for what you do for me, my family and my business."
Ernie Dell – President, Waterford, MI

"No communication can adequately convey Ron Hequet' talents."
Henry Shallcross – President, Arlington, TX

"I am fortunate to have your personal talents for my company."
Ross Hyde – President, Fort Worth, TX

"...appreciate the value of Ron's Private Mentor Program"
Craig Thoeny – CEO, Minneapolis, MN

"Ron Hequet is a trusted source...integral part of my company."
Katherine Wilson – President, Seattle, WA

"The solutions that Ron developed and implemented...are paying off."
Gary Treater – President, West Palm Beach, FL

"Ron is a very dedicated person...Ron's work is second to none."
W. James Cox – President, Portland, OR

"Ron...I'm impressed in your mission to help others...I commend you for keeping the focus where it should be...
Nate Woodbury – Owner, Lehi, UT

"Nothing as I expected, you are amazing...thank you for all that valuable information to our audience".
Ninon deVere DeRosa – CEO, Las Vegas, Nevada

"The workshop this past week with Ron Hequet was invaluable. Setting sales goals is important, but to have Ron's plan for achieving is essential".
John Leach – TSM, Kansas City, MO

"We reached $Xm this year, thank you Ron for helping us make it possible".
Pam Kruse, VP, Grand Rapids, MI

"I am very pleased to suggest that you engage Ron Hequet in your pursuit of excellence. Ron's workshops gave us the tools to see tangible improvements".
Tim Taylor – Executive Pastor, Willow Park, Texas

"We have restructured with different and more effective cost controls, and with a pre-planned profit...I feel we will recoup 2X the investment in Ron Hequet".
Gary VanSlooten, President, West Olive, MI

"Ron provided the fuel that allows common people to attain uncommon results".
Steve Thoeny – President, Crystal, MN

"You have been a blessing to me and my business".
Kevin McKee – President, Aledo, TX

Sample List Of Industries Served:

- Aero Space Parts Supply
- Advertising, Public Relations
- Apparel Manufacturing, Distribution
- Automotive Parts and Service
- Building Trades and Construction
- Computer Assembly and Service
- Commercial Vehicle Services
- Distribution Centers and Suppliers
- Electronics Sales and Marketing
- Energy Conservation
- Engineering and Design Firms
- Food Processing Industry
- EMS Claims Processing
- Healthcare and Physician Groups
- Industrial HVAC Manufacturing
- Landscape Design and Maintenance
- Machine CNC Milling Plants
- Newspapers, Publishing, Printing
- Packaging and Distribution
- Retail, Single and Multi-location
- Technology and Software Services
- Telemarketing and Sales
- Voice / Data Products and Services

...and the list goes on

Profit and Cash Flow Marketing...Fast

10 Ways to Out Think...Out Market...Out Sell Your Competition...In Any Economy

---

Special __Free__ Bonus Gifts for You!

To help you generate all the leads your business can handle, go to...

www.FreeMarketingGiftFromRon.com

✓ **Bonus 1**...2 Months Free Membership – [$194.00 value]
E-Learning Marketing System – *The Most Powerful Do-It-Yourself Customer Attraction Program Ever Created*, a 14 month program. Enroll at www.ProfitandCashMarketing.com

✓ **Bonus 2**...**Marketing Message Starter Kit** – *450 Of The Most Effective Headlines Ever Written* – [$56.00 value]

✓ **Bonus 3**...**In-depth training and motivational videos to attract more business, accomplish more goals and create more profit and cash** – [$747.00 value]

Profit and Cash Flow Marketing...Fast

PUBLISHED BY: Texas Trail, Inc.
                P.O. Box 2785
                Weatherford, Texas 76086

Copyright © 2017 by Ron Hequet, 1st Edition
Printed in the United States of America
ISBN Print Edition: 9780692843277

"Strategy without tactics is the *slowest* route to victory. Tactics without strategy is the *noise* before defeat."

— Sun Tzu

500-320 B.C., Chinese Military General, Strategist, Philosopher, Traditionally Credited As Author of 'The Art of War'

"The aim of marketing is to know and understand your customer so well, your product or service fits them and *sells itself*."

— Peter F. Drucker

1909-2005, Writer, Professor and Management Consultant

A client told me, "I don't have any money." I responded with, "I know you don't have any money, *that's why I am here*."

– Ron Hequet

Business Entrepreneur, Consultant, Speaker, Coach and author of this book

Ron Hequet

...is the ideal professional speaker for your next meeting or conference.

Dear Meeting and Event Professional:

Ron appreciates that planning and coordinating an event regardless of its size has challenges. Ron won't be one of them.

For years, **clients have entrusted him** with individual staff, teams and the entire organization, **just like yours**, to connect and **refresh, reenergize and refocus** in...strategy development, tactical planning, marketing, sales, customer service, operations, systems, team building and employee development.

What sets Ron apart is his real world experience, having owned 8 businesses in 6 different industries and having consulted to businesses in over 20 different industries.

❖ *Schedule Ron Now and Receive 100 FREE Books ($1,997.00 value) as a bonus.*

TO CONTACT AND BOOK RON TO SPEAK:
817.599.4410   Ron@RonHequet.com

6 Reasons Why Event Professionals Book Ron Hequet

✓ **Ron's personal story is inspirational**
Ron came from humble beginnings, overcoming challenges and on to a successful personal and business career.

✓ **Keeps the audience engaged**
Ron speaks from the heart and is passionate about your organization achieving results.

✓ **The audience will laugh, and be inspired to act!**
Ron will speak in his amusing style...a key point in any of Ron's messages is 'when it comes to achievement, it's not about the circumstances you see, it is what you do!', inspiring your audience to take action.

✓ **Investing in Ron = fast steps to achievement**
Through his personal experiences and proven strategies your attendees will learn how to strategically and tactically achieve higher levels of performance and results.

✓ **Ron honors all requests for a signed book**
Ron will invest time before and after the event meeting attendees and adding value to their experience and the event.

✓ **Quote cards and bookmarkers available**
Motivational cards containing quotes from Ron's talks and bookmarkers will be free to attendees.

Table of Contents

Acknowledgements

There are many people that have played a key role in my journey as a business owner, consultant, speaker, career coach and author of the book you have in your hands.

I am indebted to every client, for their trust over the past two decades, who sought me out and allowed me to develop and execute a business plan that assisted in making their business grow and become more profitable.

I also appreciate the long standing working relationships I've enjoyed with my firm's associates, whose support and expertise have greatly enhanced the value delivered to our clients.

Finally, thank you to my family, who remind me that my talents are not from anything that I have done apart from God.

Note to Reader

The accounts, case studies, names and events in this book are from over 20 years of hands-on ownership of 8 different businesses in 6 different industries, plus another 20 years of consulting to businesses in over 20 different industries. The names and settings have been altered to shield all involved, while at the same time staying true to the point and what you will learn.

Introduction

Have you ever been defeated? You start your own business to live the American dream. Things are going great for a while. Then bad stuff starts to materialize. *No matter how hard you work, no matter how many hours you put in, your dream business turns into a nightmare.*

This book is not theory or formulas gathered from research. I have based this book of business marketing and other operating principles on proven experience; the blood, sweat and tears with my own businesses and with clients' businesses, in over 20 different industries.

All of my clients have certain traits in common. First, **it takes courage just to call me**. Through our initial conversations, I hear you admit that you are unprofitable, in debt, not growing your business and that you don't know what to do about it. Finally, **you are decisive and ask for my help**.

Just by opening this book, you have already demonstrated one of those common client traits. You have taken an important step toward increasing your business success by enriching your business operating and marketing skills. **Congratulations!**

Why are the chapters titled Strategy and Tactic? "Strategic Planning" is an oxymoron. There is 'Strategy', the 'what' and 'future', and there is a 'Plan' or 'Tactics', the 'how' and 'present'.
Strategy is the targeted end game, a desired outcome and some may simply state it as the primary objective.

Definition

Strategy; is the context, in which all decisions are made that affect the character and course of the entity.

Tactic; a plan of action resulting from strategy intended to accomplish a specific goal.

The strategies and tactics in this book, when implemented with diligence, have helped businesses just like yours make tens and even hundreds of thousands of dollars…including your competitors.

This is my passion! I have dedicated my life to Business Consulting. Since starting my consulting practice to assist small business owners and entrepreneurs, occasionally I have been overwhelmed. I have found there is a great demand for someone who cares and can provide expertise and a profitable third party perspective.

It does not matter what industry or type of business you own. What matters is that you grasp the core principles, the underlying lessons and strategies in this book that can help you grow any category of business.

START NOW, not tomorrow, not next week or next year.

To your profit and cash marketing success,

Ron Hequet

PS. If you would like to arrange a meeting, in person or by phone, to get a profitable third party perspective on your business, please send an email to Ron@RonHequet.com   or   Ron@ProfitandCashMarketing.com

Strategy & Tactic 1

Define Your Target Market

What is a Target Market?

Many businesses can't answer the question: *Who is your target market?* They have often made the fatal assumption that *everyone* will want to purchase their product or service with the right marketing strategy.

A target market is simply the group of customers or clients who will purchase a specific product or service. This group of people all has something in common, often age, gender, hobbies, commercial need or location.

Your target market, then, are the people who want or need to buy your offering. This includes both existing and potential customers, all of whom are motivated to do one of three things:

✓ Fulfill a need

✓ Solve a problem

✓ Satisfy a desire

To build, maintain, and grow your business, you need to know exactly who your customers are, what they do, what they like, and why they would buy your product or service.

Getting this wrong – or not taking the time to get it right – will cost you time, money, and potentially the success of your business.

The Importance of Knowing Your Target Market

Knowledge and understanding of your target market is the keystone in the arch of your business. Without it, your product or service positioning, pricing, marketing strategy, and eventually, your business could very quickly fall apart or at least die a slow death.

If you don't intimately know your target market, you run the risk of making mistakes when it comes to establishing pricing, product mix, or service packages. Your marketing strategy will lack direction, and produce mediocre results at best. Even if your marketing message and unique selling proposition (USP) are clear, and your brochure is perfectly designed, it means nothing unless it arrives in the hands (or ears) of the right people.

Determining your target market takes time and careful diligence. While it often starts with a best guess, assumptions cannot be relied on and research is required to confirm original ideas. Your target market is not always your ideal market.

Once you build an understanding of who your target market is, keep up with your market research. Having your finger on the pulse of their motivations and drivers – which naturally change – will help you to anticipate needs or wants and evolve grow your business.

Types of Markets

Consumer

The Consumer Market includes those general consumers who buy products and services for personal use, or for use by family and friends. This is the market category you or I fall into when we're shopping for groceries or clothes, seeing a movie in the theatre, or going out for lunch. Retailers focus on this market category when marketing their goods or services.

Institutional

The Institutional Market serves society and provides products or services for the benefit of society. This includes hospitals, non-profit organizations, government organizations, schools and universities. Members of the Institutional Market purchase products to use in the provision of services to people in their care.

Business to Business (B2B)

The B2B Market is just what it seems to be: businesses that purchase the products and services of other business to run their operations.

These purchases can include products that are used to manufacture other products (raw or technical), products that are needed for daily operations (such as office supplies), or services (such as accounting, shredding, and legal).

Reseller

This market can also be called the 'Intermediary Market' because it consists of businesses that act as channels for goods and services between other markets. Goods are purchased and sold for a profit – without any alterations. Members of this market include wholesalers, retailers, resellers, and distributors.

Determining Your Target Market

Product / Service Investigation

The process for determining your target market starts by examining exactly what your offering is, and what the average customer's motivation for purchasing it is. Start by answering the following questions:

Does your offering meet a basic need?	
Does your offering serve a particular want?	
Does your offering fulfill a desire?	
What is the lifecycle of your product / service?	
What is the availability of your offering?	
What is the cost of the average customer's purchase?	
What is the lifecycle of your offering?	
How many times or how often will customers purchase your offering?	
Do you foresee any upcoming changes in your industry or region that may affect the sale of your offering (positive/negative)?	

Market Investigation

✓ **On the ground.** Spend time on the ground researching who your target market might be. If you're thinking about opening a coffee shop, hang out in the neighborhood at different times of the day to get a sense of the people who live, work, and play in the neighborhood. Notice their age, gender, clothing, and any other indications of income and activities.

✓ **At the competition.** Who is your direct competitor targeting? Is there a small niche that is being missed? Observing the clientele of your competition can help to build understanding of your target market, regardless of whether it is the same or opposite. Example: if you own a children's clothing boutique and the majority of middle-class mothers shop at the local department store, you may wish to focus on higher-income families as your target market.

✓ **Online.** Many cities and towns, or at least regions, have demographic information available online. Research the ages, incomes, occupations, and other key pieces of information about the people who live in the area you operate your business. From this data, you will gain an understanding of the size of your total potential market.

✓ **With existing customers.** Talk to your existing customers through focus groups or surveys. This is a great way to gather demographic and behavioral information, as well as feedback about product or service quality and other information that will be useful in a marketing strategy.

Who is Your Market?

Based on your product / service and market investigations, you will be able to piece together a basic picture of your target market, and some of their general characteristics. Record some notes here. At this point, you may wish to be as specific as possible, or maintain some generalities. You can further segment your market in the next section.

Consumer Target Market Framework

Market Type:	Consumer
Gender:	☐ Male ☐ Female
Age Range:	
Purchase Motivation:	☐ Meet a Need ☐ Serve a Want ☐ Fulfill a Desire
Activities:	
Income Range:	
Marital Status:	
Location:	☐ Neighborhood ☐ City ☐ Region ☐ Country
Other Notes:	

Institutional Target Market Framework

Market Type:	Institutional
Institution Type:	☐ Hospital ☐ Non-profit ☐ School ☐ University ☐ Charity ☐ Government ☐ Church
Purchase Motivation:	☐ Operational Need ☐ Client Want ☐ Client Desire
Purpose of Institution:	
Institution's Client Base:	
Size:	
Location:	☐ Neighborhood ☐ City ☐ Region ☐ Country
Other Notes:	

B2B Target Market Framework

Market Type:	Business to Business (B2B)
Company Size:	
Number of Employees:	
Purchase Motivation:	☐ Operations Need ☐ Strategy ☐ Functionality
Annual Revenue:	
Industry:	
Location(s):	
Purpose of Business:	
People, Culture & Values:	
Other Notes:	

Reseller Target Market Framework

Market Type:	Reseller
Industry:	
Client Base:	
Purchase Motivation:	☐ Operations Need ☐ Client Wants ☐ Functionality
Annual Revenue:	
Age:	
Location:	☐ Neighborhood ☐ City ☐ Region ☐ Country
Other Notes:	

Your Target Market: Putting It Together

Based on the information you gather from your product / service and market investigations, you should have a clear vision of your realistic target market. Here are a few examples of how this information is put together and conclusions are drawn:

Target Market Sample 1: Consumer Market

Business: Baby Clothing Boutique	**Business Purpose:**
Market Type: Consumer	*Meet a need* (provide clothing for infants and children aged 0 to 5 years)
Gender: Women	*Serve a want* (clothing is brand name only, and has a higher price point than the competition)
Marital Status: Married	
Market Observations: located on Main Street of Any town, a street that is seeing many new boutiques open up, proximate to the main shopping mall two blocks from popular mid-range restaurant that is busy at lunch	**Industry Predictions:** large number of new housing developments in the city and surrounding areas two new schools in construction expect to see an influx of new families move to town from Any city
Competition Observations: baby clothing also available at two local department stores, and one second-hand shop on opposite side of town	**Online Research:** half of Any town's population is female, and 25% have children under the age of 15 years Any town's population is expected to increase by 32% within three years The average household income for Any town is $75,000 annually

TARGET MARKET: The target market can then be described as married mothers with children under five years old, between the ages of 25 and 45, who have recently moved to Any-Town from Any-City, and have a household income of at least $100K annually.

Target Market Sample 2: B2B Market

Business: Confidential Paper Shredding	**Target Business Size:** Small to medium
Market Type: B2B (Business to Business)	**Target Business Revenue:** $500K to $1M
Business Purpose: *Meet an operations need* (provide confidential on-site shredding services for business documents)	**Target Business Type:** produce or handle a variety of sensitive paper documentation accountants, lawyers, real estate agents, etc.
Market Observations: there are two main areas of office buildings and industrial warehouses in Any city three more office towers are being constructed, and will be completed this year	**Industry Predictions:** the professional sector is seeing revenue growth of 24% over last year, which indicates increased client billing and staff recruitment
Competition Observations: one confidential shredding company serves the region, covering Any city and the surrounding towns provide regular (weekly or biweekly) service, but does not have the capacity to handle large volumes at one time	**Online Research:** Any city's biggest employment sectors are: manufacturing, tourism, food services, and professional services

TARGET MARKET:

The target market can then be described as small to medium sized businesses in the professional sector with annual revenue of $500K to $1M who require both regular and infrequent large volume paper shredding services.

Segmenting Your Market

Your market segments are the groups within your target market – broken down by a determinant in one of the following four categories:

✓ Demographics

✓ Psychographics

✓ Geographic

✓ Behaviors

Segmenting your target market into several more specific groups allows you to further tailor your marketing campaign and more specifically position your product or service. You may wish to divide your ad campaign into four sections, and target four specific markets with messages that will most resonate with the audience.

For example, the baby clothing store may choose to segment its target market by psychographics, or lifestyle. If the larger target market is *married females with children under five, between the ages of 25 and 45, who have a household income of at least $100K annually*, it can be broken down into the following lifestyle segments:

✓ Fitness-oriented mothers

✓ Career-oriented mothers

✓ New mothers

With these three categories, unique marketing messages can be created that speak to the hot-buttons of each segment. The more accurate and specific you can make communications with your target market, the greater impact you will have on your revenues.

Market Segmentation Variables

Demographic	Psychographic	Geographic	Behavioristic
Age	Personality	Region	Brand Loyalty
Income	Lifestyle	Country	Product Usage
Gender	Values	City	Purchase
Generation	Attitude	Area	Frequency
Nationality	Motivation	Neighborhood	Profitability
Ethnicity	Activities	Density	Readiness to Buy
Marital Status	Interests	Climate	User Status
Family Size			
Occupation			
Religion			
Language			
Education			
Employment Type			
Housing Type			
Housing Ownership			
Political Affiliation			

Understanding Your Target Market

Once you have determined who your market is, make a point of learning everything you can about them. You need to have a strong understanding of who they are, what they like, where they shop, why they buy, and how they spend their time. Remind yourself that you may *think* you know your market, but until you have verified the information, you'll be driving your marketing strategy blind.

Also be aware that markets change, just like people. Just because you knew your market when you started your business 10 years ago, doesn't mean you know it now. Regular market research is part of any successful business plan, and a great habit to start.

Types of Market Research

Surveys

The simplest way to gather information from your clients or target market is through a survey. You can craft a questionnaire full of questions about your product, service, market demographics, buyer motivations, and so on. Plus, anonymous surveys will produce the most accurate information since names are not attached to the results or specific comments.

Depending on the purpose—whether it is to gather demographic information, product or service feedback, or other data—there are a number of ways to administer a survey.

- *Telephone*

Telephone surveys are a more time-consuming option, but have the benefit of live communication with your target market. Generally, it is best to have a third party conduct this type of survey to gather the most honest feedback. This is the method that market researchers use for polling, which is highly reliable.

- *Online*

Online surveys are the easiest to administer yourself. There are many web-based services that quickly and easily allow to you custom create your survey, and send it to your email marketing list. These services can also analyze, summarize and interpret the results on your behalf. Keep in mind that the results include only those who are motivated to respond, which may slant your results.

- *Paper-based*

Paper surveys are seldom used, and can prove to be an inefficient method. Like online surveys, your results are based on the feedback of those who were motivated for one reason or another to respond. However, the time and effort involved in taking the survey, filing it out, and returning it to your place of business may deter people from participating.

Keep in mind that surveys can be complex to administer, and consume more time and resources than you have planned. If you have the budget, consider hiring a professional market research firm to lead or assist with the process. This will also ensure that the methodology is standard practice, and will garner the most accurate results.

Website Analysis

Tracking your website traffic is an excellent way to research your existing and potential customer's interests and behavior. From this information, you can ensure the design, structure and content of your website is catering to the people who use it – and the people you want to use it.

User-friendly website traffic analytics programs can easily show you who are visiting your site, where they are from, and what pages of your site they are viewing. Services like Google Analytics can tell you what page they arrive at, where they click to, how much time they spend on each page, and on which page they leave the site.

This is powerful (and free!) information to have in your market research, and easy to monitor monthly or weekly, depending on the needs of your business.

Customer Purchase Data (Consumer Behavior)

If you do not have the budget to conduct your own professional market research, you can use existing resources on consumer behavior. While this data may not be specific to your region or city, general consumer research is actual data that can be helpful in confirming assumptions you may have made about your target market.

Your customer loyalty program or Point of Sale system may also be of help in tracking customer purchases and identifying trends in purchase behavior. If you can track who is buying, what they're buying and how often they're buying, you'll have an arsenal of powerful insight into your existing client base.

Focus Groups

Focus groups look at the psychographic and behavioristic aspects of your target market. Groups of six to 12 people are gathered and asked general and specific questions about their purchase motivations and behaviors. These questions could relate to your business in particular, or to the general industry.

Focus group sessions can also be time consuming to organize and facilitate, so consider hiring the services of a professional market research firm. You may also receive more honest information if a third party is asking the questions, and receiving the responses from focus group participants.

For cost savings, consider partnering with an associate in the same industry who is not a direct competitor, and who would benefit from the same market data.

Ron's Journal 1:

One of my early consulting clients, located in Lubbock, Texas, was a copier / printer repair business, doing about 5MM, but barely staying in business. Suffering from low margins, job cost overruns and other related issues, the owner had almost no return.

I discovered they also refilled printer cartridges as an add-on sale for any Tom-Dick or Harriet that walked through the door with a single cartridge for their at home printer. **It was the most profitable single sales item in the business.** Profitable – but a time-suck.

While reorganizing the overall business operations, to eliminate certain types of customer's work, improving margins, eliminating job cost overruns, et al, I analyzed the cartridge refill part of the business (because of its profit potential), using the charts in this chapter and found their target market to be B2B. We targeted every bank, law firm, accounting firm, Texas Tech University or similar business. That's where the volume was in this case.

I asked the owner, "Would you rather have your existing 5MM in gross revenue with a .05% net operating profit (NOP), or would you like to have a 3.5MM business with a 9% NOP?" You do the math.

Strategy & Tactic 2

Profits from Fresh Air

As a small business owner, you are in business for the primary reason: **to make money.**

Of course, there are other reasons you started or purchased your company. You may love the product you sell, or service you provide. You may love the challenge of turning a floundering company into an overnight success. You may just love being your own boss.

Naturally, this all means nothing if you are not generating enough income to support yourself and your family, as well as the people who work for you.

Nearly all businesses make money. Unless not a single product or service is sold, there is always money coming in. But there is also always money going out. Supplies, wages, marketing, acquisitions and operations all contribute to the expense of just staying in business.

Simply put, profit is the difference between money in and money out. This is the dollar value of your sales, minus the cost of those sales.

In business, you will find that everyone wants to make more money. They want to increase their sales, get more money coming in. **What often gets overlooked is that the true secret to making more money is not increasing sales, but increasing profit.**

What is Profit?

Before you can take steps to increase the profitability of your business, you have to have a solid understanding of:

✓ types of profit

✓ what factors influence profit

✓ what your profit is *right now*

Types of Profit

There are two main types of profit:

Gross Profit

Gross profit is the simplest form of calculating profit. It is simply the money that comes through the cash register, minus the cost of acquiring or providing the products or services.

The formula is:

Total revenue (sales) – cost of goods or services sold = Gross Profit

Net Profit

Net profit is a more accurate reflection of your income. It is calculated by taking your gross profit minus expenses over a specific time period (usually by quarter).

The formula is:

Gross profit – expenses (cost of running a business) = Net Profit

Factors that Influence Profit

Profit is your bottom line. It is the number that falls out the bottom when all other costs and expenses have been taken into consideration. Do you know what contributes to the amount of profit your business ends up with?

There are three main factors that influence profit:

Sales – Your Conversion Rate

The first, and most obvious, factor is the money that comes in the door through sales. In theory, the more sales you make, the more money you bring in, the greater your profits.

The ratio of potential customers to sales is called your conversion rate. This is the percentage of customers you have converted from leads to sales. So, a high conversion rate means more sales, and more money coming in the door.

In addition to your conversion rate is the lifetime value of your clients. It costs much less to convince a customer to make repeat purchases than it does to acquire new clients.

Costs – Your Product/Service Margins

The second factor is the cost of your offering – what your product or service costs you to acquire or provide. If you sell a product, this is the wholesale price you pay for the product. If you offer a service, it is the cost of your (or your employee's) time plus any materials used.

Your margin is the difference between the price you pay and the price your customers pay. If you buy toothpaste for $1 from the wholesaler, and you sell it for $3, your margin is $2. If a haircut costs $20 in materials and service, and the customer pays $50, your margin is $30.

Expenses – The Cost of Doing Business

The final factor is the cost of running your business – those not directly related to the specific product or service you offer. Expenses include:

✓ Office or store lease
✓ Computer equipment lease
✓ Employee salaries
✓ Utilities
✓ Marketing + advertising

Your Profit

It only makes sense that you need to know where you are to determine how to get to where you want to be. This applies to any plan to create in business.

Before you can increase your profits, you need to have an understanding of where your profits are currently – and if you're making any at all. The next section will take you through a process to review the specific factors that affect your business's profitability, and ultimately determine how much profit you are currently bringing in.

Taking Stock of Your Profits

Before you devise a strategy to increase your profits, you need to take a good long look at the money your business brings in, and the money you spend to run your business. Decide on a specific time period to review – one that makes sense to your business, and one that will give you the most realistic picture of your business performance.

This will depend on if your operation is cyclical, or remains steady throughout the year. Usually, the previous quarter or the previous four quarters will give you enough of an indication.

Here is a general list of items to review:

- ✓ Total revenue
- ✓ Total cost of goods or services
- ✓ Total cost of operations (overhead), including:
- ✓ Employee wages
- ✓ Recruitment
- ✓ Business development
- ✓ Utilities
- ✓ Rent or mortgage
- ✓ Office supplies
- ✓ Computer leases
- ✓ Incidentals
- ✓ Total cost of marketing campaigns

Total profit after costs and expenses for this time period:

$_____.

The Five Factors that Eat Your Profits

It is easy for business owners to compare their organizations to the apparent success of their competitors. Joe's Pizza may always be teaming with customers and appear to be making money hand over fist, while your pizza shop may have slower, but a more consistent business.

It is important to remember that a business with extraordinary sales figures is not necessarily a profitable one. Sales are just one element of your profit calculation.

Much of my consulting career has been developing strategies, teaching business owners and implementing processes and procedures to make their business profitable at their *current* sales level first – not trying to increase sales.

Here are some other elements to think about when reviewing the profitability of your business:

Impulse Spending

How often do you make purchases for your business operations? I'm not talking about acquiring new goods and services, but upgrading computers, taking your team out for lunch, or leasing a new color photocopier.

Do you allow your staff to make purchases on your behalf? Who reviews these decisions? Take a look not only at *what* you buy, but *how* spending is structured in your company.

Small Margins

As we discussed in the previous section, your margins are the difference between your cost and the customer's cost to purchase your goods or services.

Typically, businesses that offer a variety of products will have both products with large margins, and products with small margins. The products with large margins generate the most income, so these are the products that staff should be focused on selling.

What many businesses overlook is that products with small margins will never generate a high level of income, no matter how many you sell. A store stocked with small margin items will never be able to increase their profit because they have so little margin to work with.

Your Customers

This may seem like a backwards way of thinking. Your customers spend money, so they are a positive factor in your profit calculation, right?

This is true for most of your customers. But remember the 80/20 rule of business – 80% of your revenue comes from 20% of your customers. These are your top 20%, or ideal customers. What about your bottom 20%? This is the group of clients who ask for the moon and never stop complaining.

These clients can be a huge drain on both your staff resources and your financial resources. Their true value to your business is minimal – they cost more than they bring in. Fire them!

Loan Interest

How many business loans do you currently have? Credit card debit? Overdraft? The interest you pay on these loans can be a substantial monthly cost to your business.

A loan from a bank is just like any other product. You can shop around for the best deal. Consider consolidating or restructuring your debt to minimize interest payments. Plan to search around for the best rate on a regular basis – every few months or quarter.

Vendors

Do you purchase your goods and services from a wholesaler or retailer? How long have you been in business with this company? What do you pay for goods and services relative to your competitors?

Ensure that you are dealing with as direct a vendor as possible to minimize your acquisition costs and increase your margins. If you have been doing business with a particular vendor for an extended period of time, consider renegotiating your business arrangement.

The Basics of Increasing Profit

Your Profitability Goal

Now that you have an understanding of the current profitability of your company, it is time to look at ways to increase your bottom line.

Like all other aspects of your business development, you need to have a clear idea of your intention or purpose before you begin any activity. Assuming you wish to increase the profitability of your business, you need to determine by how much and within what time frame.

Create a profit-related goal for your business, and write it here:

_____

_____

_____

_____

_____

Three Ways to Increase Profit

There are countless strategies for increasing profit, but ultimately you can only increase profit in one of three ways:

1. Get More Customers

Use marketing outreach strategies to generate more leads, and convert those leads into more customers. Introduce a new offer, expand your target audience, or approach a new target audience.

2. Get Your Customers to Buy More Often

Use customer loyalty and retention strategies to get your existing customers to buy from you more often. Make it easy for them to come back and do business with you.

You can do this by adding value to your product or service, keeping in touch on a regular basis, and giving your customers incentive to make repeat purchases. Customer service is also an overlooked component of building a repeat client base.

3. Increase How Much Your Customers Buy

You'll naturally increase your sales when you increase the number of customers and how often they purchase. The final way you can impact your profit is by increasing the average dollar value of each sale.

This can be achieved by up-selling every customer, creating package offers, and finding ways to increase the perceived value of your offering to justify increasing the price.

Managing Costs

One important way to impact the profitability of your business is through cost or spending management. Controlling how much money goes out will help you ensure that more money stays in your bank account.

Remember, however, that cutting costs can only help increase your profits so much. There is a point where you will no longer be able to reduce expenses, and you will have to focus on increasing sales.

Why Cut Costs?

Cost management may seem like an obvious way of maintaining a healthy business, but it is also one of the primary reasons 80% of small businesses fail. Overspending is a huge problem for most businesses – and they don't even realize it.

Reducing costs is a great short-term strategy to boost profits. As I mentioned above, there is a limited amount of impact cost management can have on the bottom line, so it is an ineffective long term strategy.

Cost management can also help you to generate more capital. A business that closely monitors and controls its spending is a much more desirable loan candidate than a business that spends freely.

Most importantly, this strategy will help keep your business profitable through high and low periods. It's easy to spend money when your company is doing well, but this leaves little in the "just in case" account for downturns in the economy or unexpected expenses.

Where Can I Cut Costs?

Financing

As I mentioned, interest rates are a big culprit when it comes to eating profits. Take stock of how much money you are spending on a monthly basis in loan and interest payments. Can this be reduced? Is there another bank that will offer you a lower rate? Is there a way to consolidate these loans into a single, low-interest account?

Alternatively, if your business is doing well and has a large amount of money sitting in the bank; consider investing it or placing it in a high-interest savings account. Let your money make you money instead of spending it on unnecessary business luxuries.

Suppliers or Vendors

Again, as mentioned above, make sure the price you pay for goods and services – for resale or internal use – is the lowest you can find. Try to deal directly with the manufacturer or distributor, and renegotiate discounts and contracts with your vendors every year.

Hours of Operation

Evaluate the hours you are open for business each day, and why you have chosen the specific timeframe. Is it to compete with the competitors? Is it because you can serve the highest number of customers? Each hour you are open for business costs you money, so make sure you are operating under the most ideal timeframe.

Staffing, Wages, and Compensation

This can be a sensitive subject for any business owner or employee. It is important to look at staffing redundancies and capacity levels – as well as hiring needs – when evaluating cost management strategies.

Do you need to hire new staff, or can you build capacity within your existing employees? Is there another way to compensate staff, or provide performance incentives that are non-monetary, have a high perceived value, and inexpensive for your business? Remember to take time and care when implementing any changes in this area of cost management.

Place of Business

If you operate an office in a downtown metropolis, you are going to have substantially higher operating costs than a competitor who runs an office just outside the city limits.

Make sure you can justify your location, and the amount of money you spend to be there. Consider the following questions:

- ✔ Are my customers impacted by where I do business?
- ✔ Do my customers need to visit my office?
- ✔ What impression does my business need to present?
- ✔ Do I need parking facilities?
- ✔ Do I need to be visible?
- ✔ Do I have staff to employ?

✓ Am I near public transit, lunch outlets, and other amenities?

✓ Do I need access after business hours?

✓ Should I lease or buy?

✓ What other costs are specific to this location?

Eliminate the invisible!

What could you and your staff live without? What wouldn't you notice if it just disappeared one day? Take stock of expenses that are not being properly used or appreciated. Think of amenity-based items, or convenience costs, like:

✓ Gym Memberships

✓ Morning refreshments (muffins, donuts, etc.)

✓ Publication Subscriptions

✓ Designer coffee and tea

✓ Fancy collateral packaging

Your Pricing Strategy

The cost of your goods and services has a direct impact on the money you bring in. Your pricing strategy is so important to your business that can even determine your success.

Deciding how much to charge for your product or service is a challenging task. You need to factor in your own costs, the product or service's perceived value, and the going rate. Ultimately, you want to be able to charge as much as possible for each item, without overpricing yourself out business.

Avoid the Lowest Pricing Strategy

The days of the lowest price guarantee and pricing wars are over – especially for small businesses. The "big players" in the marketplace will quickly put you out of business if you try to compete on price. Their pockets are deeper and they have lower operating costs due to their sheer size. They can afford to – you can't.

Clearly Position Your Company and Your Offering

How do you want your target market to view your business, and your products? Are you trying to create an image of high quality? High value? Reliable service? Make sure your pricing is consistent with the image you are trying to project. If you are operating a high end spa – you're not competing with the budget nail salon down the street, so your prices should be considerably higher.

Have a Good Working Understanding of Your Margins

Know how much the product or service costs you to offer before you establish a price. Do these costs remain consistent, or do they fluctuate? Restaurants that offer high quality meat and seafood often price their meals at "market rates" as opposed to fixed rates. Calculate the fixed and variable costs associated with your product or service. You will want to work the cost of the product or service, a percentage of your overhead, and your own profit into the cost of each item.

Pay Attention to Factors beyond Your Control

Be aware of any government or industry regulations on the price of your product or services. Some laws will actually limit how much you can charge for standard services. For medical and dental services, most insurance companies will put a cap on how much a customer will be compensated for each service. Seek out all external factors that could impact your pricing.

Price with a Purpose

Your pricing strategy should be purpose focused. What exactly are you trying to do by setting your prices at certain levels? Here are some potential reasons for pricing strategies:

- ✔ Short-term profit increase
- ✔ Long-term profit increase
- ✔ Customer generation
- ✔ Product positioning
- ✔ Revenue maximization
- ✔ Increase margins
- ✔ Market differentiation
- ✔ Survival

Pricing Strategies

Cost plus Pricing

This is the most basic pricing strategy. Set your price at a number that includes:

- ✔ Cost of goods or services, based on a specific sales volume
- ✔ Percentage of expenses
- ✔ Profit margin (markup)

Target ROI Pricing

Set your price at a rate that will achieve a specific Return on Investment target. If you need to make $20,000 from 1,000 units – or $20 per unit – then set your price at $20 more than cost, plus expenses.

Value Based Pricing

This can be a bit of an arbitrary pricing strategy, but it can also be the most profitable. Set your price based on the value or added benefit it brings to a customer. For example, if your product only costs you $40 to produce, but will save the customer $2,000 per year in energy costs; a price of $150 or $200 would not appear to be unreasonable in the eyes of the customer.

Psychological Pricing

What messages are you trying to send the customer when they're looking at your prices for your products? Do you offer the best deal? The highest value? These are reasons to choose prices that are higher or lower than the competition.

Pricing Guidelines

Price higher than cost: This may seem obvious, but ensure that your pricing not only covers your costs, but potential fluctuations in sales volume and in the marketplace. If you sell half of your order, will you still make a profit?

Include expenses: If you price to cover your costs, will you also be able to cover your expenses and still see a profit? Your margin needs to pay for your expenses, leave you with something to live on, plus some working capital for the company.

Consider the 'fair' price: What do your consumers think is 'fair' for each service or product? This is impacted by your competitor's price, your company's image (high quality or high value, low cost), and the perceived value of your product or service.

Strategies to Increase Profit

Once you have a concrete understanding of where your business stands today in terms of profitability, minimized your operating costs, and restructured your pricing strategy, you can focus on other strategies to increase profit.

There are countless strategies and tactics that will help you to bring in more customers, get those customers to come back, and get those customers to spend more when they do.

Here is a list of ideas, many of which are covered in detail in other sections of this program:

- ✓ Advertise
- ✓ Establish an online presence
- ✓ Sell more high margin items
- ✓ Generate more leads
- ✓ Focus on referral business
- ✓ Increase customer loyalty and repeat business
- ✓ Increase conversion rates
- ✓ Restructure your team
- ✓ Reinvent your product
- ✓ Sell your intellectual capital

Ron's Journal No. 2:

A sales and distribution business in Kansas City with sales of about 25M had a loss of 800K+. By the way; this problem existed with clients over the years that had gross revenues of 2.5MM down to 250K. Don't in any way compare your business to others. Size doesn't matter when it comes to operating and growing your business in a profitable way. I'd rather have a small company that was profitable, with good cash flow, than a big one that was broke.

After I completed a thorough analysis of the entire company, I demonstrated what it would take to turn this company around and the investment it would require.

Before hiring me (thinking they would save money), they made an attempt to increase sales, believing that would solve their problem. They did increase sales by a few hundred thousand, but still lost money. They didn't fix what was wrong with their company first.

They couldn't make their loan payments, receivables grew exponentially and the bank was talking as if they were going to 'call the note'.

The owners called me for help to save their business. There's not enough space here to describe the strategy and all the tactical action steps that were executed, but over a period of time, the business was doing a little less than 25MM, but with a net operating profit of 1.2MM.

Strategy & Tactic 3

Create Added Value in Your Business and Make 1 + 1 = 3

The majority of small businesses, like yours, are established in response to market demand for a product or service. Many build their businesses by serving that demand, and enjoy growing profits without putting much effort into long-term planning or marketing.

However, what happens when that demand slows or stops? What happens when the competition sets up shop with a "new and improved" version of your product down the road? How do you keep your offering fresh, while growing and maintaining your client base? The answer is by adding value to your product or service.

Added value is a marketing or customer relations strategy that can take the form of a product, service, which is added to the original offering for free, or as part of a discounted package. It, like all other elements in your marketing toolkit, is designed to attract new customers and retain existing ones. A simple example of added value would be if you owned a gift shop, and offered complimentary gift wrapping with every purchase.

If you don't refresh and renew your offering over time, your customers will get bored and be drawn to your competitor. Your employees, too, may become disinterested, and find work elsewhere. Ultimately, both clients and employees will demand additional value to remain loyal – and aren't they the keystones for your business growth?

Can You Add Value to Your Business?

Everyone can add value to their business. Better yet, everyone can *afford* to add value to their business. Adding value doesn't have to blow your marketing budget, or take up hours of your time. There are many ways – big and small – to enhance your business in the eyes of your clients.

The key to adding value is determining what your customers and target market perceive as valuable. You must understand their needs, wants, troubles and inconveniences in order to entice them with solutions through added value products or services. Adding value will add to your profits, but if you don't focus on genuinely helping your clients, you'll have a difficult time attracting them.

Added value works for both product- and service-based businesses. If you offer a service, like hairstyling, try treating your customers with products like a latte while they wait, shampoo samples, or a free conditioning treatment with every sixth visit. If you sell a product, consider offering convenience services – like free shipping or delivery – to make the customer's experience a seamless one. The customer will feel appreciated and their needs will have been taken care of.

Ways to Add Value to Your Business

There are many ways to enhance your offer, depending on your budget and the resources you have access to. You may wish to hold a brainstorming session with your staff to come up with ideas for your business; if your employees are on the front lines, they'll likely have firsthand information about what clients would like to see more of.

Feature Your Expertise

Your intellectual property is a free resource that you have at your disposal to share with your clients. This will make them feel as though they have an inside track. You might want to consider adding it to your business, making it a value-added service.

Expert corner: Supplement your website and newsletter with columns on topics of interest to your customers and of relevance to your service. This will position you as an expert in the marketplace, and give your clients helpful information they won't receive from the competition.

Do It Yourself Tips: This is a great tool for seasonal marketing. Provide your clients with this information on your website, in your newsletters, or on take away note cards in your store or office. Ideas include recipes, craft ideas, gift ideas – all of which are branded with your company logo and contact information, and include your product as an ingredient.

What to Expect Tips: Take your customer through what they should expect in the first few days (weeks) of using your service or product, and how they can make the most of it. This can include assembly instructions, product care and cleaning, or service results (like a 25% increase in business – guaranteed!).

Related + Community Events: Own a store that sells athletic equipment? Post information on your website, in store, and in your newsletter about upcoming races, games, or consumer trade shows. Or simply keep a bulletin in your office of community events and offers that will draw your clients in, and establish it as a hub in the neighborhood for information.

Offer Convenience Services

Customer service is a dying practice in our high paced culture – use it to your advantage. When done well, it can be the difference between you and the competition, or the deciding factor for a potential repeat client.

Envision the steps involved for a customer to arrive at your store, purchase your offering, and use your product or service. Can you eliminate any of those steps for them? Can you shorten waiting times, or make them more pleasurable? Stepping into your clients' shoes will allow you to determine the most powerful value add for your company. Here are a few ideas:

Free Delivery + Shipping: With clearly established parameters (will you ship your product free to India?); this is a solid value added service that many businesses offer.

Free delivery (usually with a purchase over a set amount) is a huge convenience for many people who do not have access to a vehicle, or need help moving large items.

Follow up Services: This works great for computers, appliances and other mechanical or technology-based products. Offer maintenance and service contracts for three time periods; instead of dealing with the manufacturer, customers will rely on you for assistance which brings them back into the store and establishes a relationship of trust.

Gift-Wrapping: A great service to provide – especially for seasonal gifts. This service costs very little, and can have a big impact on your customer's experience.

'While You Wait' Amenities: If you could make your customer feel like a VIP for minimal cost, why wouldn't you? Offering amenities like coffee and treats, free samples and services (wireless internet is a big one) will go a long way.

Comparison-Shopping Tools: Show your customers that you are so sure your product will measure up against the competition, which you'll help them compare.

Establish Complementary Partnerships

Complementary partnerships with other businesses can take you a long way toward adding value for your customer, and generating new business. Just like a joint testimonial mailing, the power (and convenience) of referral business is immense.

Build a web of associates: If you're a yoga instructor, carry the cards of your treatment providers (physiotherapists, massage therapists, etc.) to refer your students to. In exchange, your brochure or card is posted in their offices. This works for automotive repair, esthetics, consultants and other service providers. Customers will trust referrals received by their existing service providers, and feel taken care of by a reputable community of experts.

Establish partnerships with financial incentives: This is one that has your interests in mind as well as your customers'. In addition to establishing a complementary partnership with a related associate, establish an incentive structure where each of you is compensated for your referrals. For example, if you refer a client to a furniture store after they've purchased a mattress from you, and they buy a bed frame, your associate will pay you a portion of the sale – and vice versa.

Location-based partnerships: Consider creating partnerships with the businesses around you – even if your products and services don't appear to be related. Shopping malls do this all the time with value coupon books that customers must purchase for $5 to $20 dollars. These partnerships and incentives will keep the customer spending money in the area, which is good for everyone's bottom line.

Packages + Bundles

Packaging and bundling products and services is one of the most popular methods of adding value. Clients perceive the bundles as having a higher value than the sum of the individual items – or as receiving something for free.

Cleverly packaged and named bundles can spark interest and revive your products in the eyes of your customers. Remember to always give the offers an end date or provide a limited number to create a sense of scarcity and urgency and to prevent this strategy from going stale.

Intuitive product bundles: Package independent related products together, and give them a reduced price or name. For example, this could be selling an extra pair of running socks with new running shoes. Remember the convenience of starter kits – package everything your customer will need to begin a new activity – painting, camping, running, etc. – in a bundle for simple buying decisions.

Package your upsell: This can also be called a chain of purchasing. It includes the products or services your client will need to use your product or service. Won't they need leather protector for their new boots? If they've run out of oil paints, how's their supply of brushes, acrylics or canvases? By packaging these clearly related products together, you are making their shopping experience faster and more convenient.

Offer a Customer Loyalty Program

There are a number of ways to structure your rewards and loyalty program, depending on the type of business and level of technological resources available to you. Customer loyalty programs have a huge advantage – they help build your database of customer information and in most cases allow you to view and analyze purchasing patterns. Here are the most popular:

Every 6th (or 10th) Visit on Us: This works well for business that rely on repeat visits from their customers – like hair salons, coffee shops, auto maintenance, etc. Customers receive a card with store information on the front, and space for stamps or initials on the back. Remember that while 10 is a nice even number, it may be too far in the future for some customers (especially for services that are three to six weeks apart). The idea of six visits is more manageable.

Rewards Dollars: This is the Canadian Tire model. For every dollar your customer spends in store, they receive a small portion back in store credit (i.e., Canadian Tire money). The store credit is in the form of printed dollars, branded with your company logo and contact information, and serves as a reminder each time a client opens their wallet.

Rewards Points: Another common value-add strategy is a rewards points system. Most grocery stores use this incentive, as well as credit card companies. This works the same as rewards dollars, where a certain number of points are accumulated based on each dollar spent in store. Points can then be spent in store, or on products you have brought in for "rewards points holders" only. This strategy also allows you to feature products with "extra point's value" instead of discounting prices.

Membership Amenities: Instead of points or dollars, you can offer VIP treatment for members, when they sign up for or purchase a membership. This may include occasional discounts, but is primarily centered around perks like "while you wait" amenities, skipping the line, free delivery, etc. You can also produce membership cards.

Ron's Journal No. 3:

Years ago I was called in to fix an auto-body shop in Oklahoma, with some of the common small business problems of cash flow, low margins, and operational disorganization, resulting in the owner involved in every transaction, from checking in a vehicle, managing the repair process, to completing the transaction with the customer.

When I arrived, I was given a tour of the facility. The outside appearance was good but nothing special, *but inside*…my eyes bugged out when I saw at least a half dozen NASCAR race cars being worked on, in addition to dozens of family vehicles you and I might drive. Turns out, the owner of this business had a reputation and a special relationship with many of the owners of these race cars and they wanted no one else to work on them but him.

Correcting the consulting project issues was easily accomplished in less than a month. Why; the owner and key staff were receptive to and wanted to learn to do it all, the right way. **The challenge was growing the business.**

I asked the owner, "Do the people in this market know about your relationship to NASCAR?"

Guess what, I used many of the tactics in this chapter to market and grow his business, which doubled over the next 10 months.

Strategy & Tactic 4

How to Create Repeat Business and Have Clients that Pay, Stay and Refer

When it comes to marketing and generating more income, most business owners are focused outward.

They've carefully established and segmented their target market, and created specific offers and messages for each market segment. They spend thousands of dollars in advertising and direct mail campaigns in hot pursuit of more leads, more customers, and more foot traffic.

While this is an effective way to build a business, it is costly and time consuming. It requires constant and consistent effort, and while this approach does generate results, those results quickly disappear when the effort stops or becomes less intense.

Successful businesses that see sustained growth have a double-edged marketing strategy. They focus their efforts *outward* – on new potential customers and marketing – as well as *inward* – on existing customers and referral business.

These successful businesses have leveraged their existing efforts to generate more revenue. Simply put, their customers buy from them over and over again.

For most businesses, this is the easiest way to increase their revenues. Simple customer loyalty strategies and outstanding customer service are often all you need to dramatically increase your sales – from the customers you already have.

The Cost of Your Customers

Do you know how much it costs your business to buy new customers?

Each new customer that walks through your door – with the exception of referrals – has cost you money to acquire. You have spent money on advertising and promotions to generate leads and turn those leads into customers.

For example, if you have placed an ad in your local newspaper for $1,000, and the ad brings in 10 customers, you have paid $100 to acquire each customer. You would need to ensure each of those customers spent at least $200 to cover your margin and break even. Alternately, if you spent two hours of your time and $10 per month on an email marketing program to send a newsletter to your existing database of customers, and you bring in 10 customers as a result – each customer has cost you $1.

Generating more repeat business means focusing on the marketing strategies that aim to keep your existing customers instead of purchase new ones – effectively reducing the cost of attracting new customers to your business.

These strategies are simple to implement, and don't require much time investment. Just a solid understanding of how to make customers want to come back and spend more of their money

Keeping Your Customers

Marketing strategies that focus on keeping your current customer base are easy and enjoyable to implement. They allow you to build real relationships with the people you do business with, instead of dealing with a revolving door of people on the other end of your sales process.

Repeat customers create a community of people around your business that presumably share the same needs, desires and frustrations. The information you gain from these customers (market research) can help you strengthen your understanding of your target audience, and more accurately segment it.

Remember – 80% of your revenue comes from 20% of your customers. Always focus on these customers. They are ideal customers that you want to recruit, and hold on to.

Customer Service: Make them love buying from you

Every business – even those with excellent service standards can improve the service they provide their customers. Customer service seems to be a dying concept in most businesses; more focus seems to be placed on the speed of the transaction. These days you can even go to the grocery store now and not speak to a single sales associate thanks to self-serve checkouts.

To improve your company's customer service standards, take a survey of your customers and your employees to brainstorm ways you can improve the experience of buying from your business.

Successful customer service standards – those that make your customers *buy* – are:

Consistent: The standards are up kept by every person in your organization. Expectations are clear and followed through. Customers know what to expect, and choose your business because of those expectations.

Convenient: It is nearly effortless for the customer to spend money at your place of business. Convenience can take many forms – location, product selection, value-added services like delivery – and it is also consistent.

Customer-driven: The service the customer receives is exactly how they would like to be treated when buying your product or service. It is reflective of your target market, and appropriate to their lifestyle. Customers would probably not appreciate white linen tablecloths at a fast food restaurant, but they would appreciate a 2-minutes or less guarantee.

Newsletters: Keep in touch with your customers

A regular newsletter is an easy, time-effective, and inexpensive marketing strategy to implement. Unfortunately, many small businesses think these are too time consuming and too expensive to adopt as part of their marketing strategy.

The most popular type of newsletter distribution is email. This will cost your business as little at $10 per month for an email marketing service subscription, and can be customized to your unique branding.

Here is an easy five-step process to starting a company newsletter:

1. Pick your audience: New customers? Market segment? Existing customers?

2. Choose what you're going to say: Company news? Feature product? New offer?

3. Determine how you're going to say it: Articles? Bullet points? Pictures?

4. Decide how it's going to get to your audience: Email? Mail? In-store?

5. Track your results: How many people opened it? Read it? Took action?

Value Added Service: Give them happy surprises

Adding value to your business is an effective way of getting your customers back. Every person I know would choose a mattress store that offered free delivery over one that did not. It's that simple.

There are many ways to add value to your business, including:

✓ **Feature your expertise:** Use your knowledge to provide additional value to your customers. Offer a free consumer guide or report with every purchase.

✓ **Add convenience services:** Offer a service that makes their purchase easier, or more convenient. The best example of this is free shipping or delivery.

✓ **Package complementary services**: Packaging like items together creates an increase in perceived value. This is great for start-up kits.

✓ **Offer new products or services:** Feature top of the line or exclusive products, available only at your business. Offer a new service or profile a new staff member with niche expertise.

Value added services generate repeat customers in one of two ways:

1. Impress them on their first visit. Impress you customer with great service, a product that meets their needs, and then wow them with something extra that they weren't expecting. Get them to associate the experience of dealing with your business with happy surprises, and create a perception of higher value.

2. Entice them to come back. The introduction of a new value-added service can be enough to convince a customer to buy from you again. Their initial purchase established a trust and knowledge of your business and its processes. They will want to "be included" in anything new you have to offer – especially if there is exclusivity. It is easier to attract clients that have purchased from you than potential clients who have not.

Customer Loyalty Programs: Give them incentives

Another simple way to keep in touch with existing customers and keep them coming back to you is to create a customer loyalty program.

These programs do not have to be complicated or costly, and are relatively easy to maintain once they have been implemented. These programs help you gain more information on your customers and their purchasing habits.

Here are some examples of simple loyalty programs that you can implement:

Free product or service: Give them every 10th (or 6th) product or service free. Produce stamp cards with your logo and contact information on it.

Reward dollars: Give them a certain percentage of their purchase back in money that can only be spent in-store. Produce "funny money" with your logo and brand.

Rewards points: Give them a certain number of points for every dollar they spend. These points can be spent in-store, or on special items you bring in for points only.

Membership amenities: Give members access to VIP amenities that are not available to other customers. Produce member cards or give out member numbers.

Remember that in order for this strategy to work, you and your team have to understand and promote it. The program in itself becomes a product that you sell.

Ron's Journal No. 4:

A florist in Maryland called me because the business had come to a halt in terms of growth. Sales were flat for the last few years, and with annual operating cost increases, which all businesses experience, **profit was dwindling** to say the least. Their lack of a marketing plan was the primary issue.

I first developed and conducted an employee training program; everything from how to answer and use the phone, greeting and consulting with customers, to merchandising and the packaging of products.

Next, we implemented many of the tactics in this chapter, and **one in particular, we called *'The Men's Club'*.**

There's not enough space here to list all of the benefits of the program, but for instance, when a man signed up, he received advance notice of every anniversary, birthday, Valentine's Day, holiday, Mother's Day, special event and anything else he put on his list. He received the gifts and flowers he chose in advance or could make another choice. The 'Club' included discounts, delivery options, special wrapping and much more.

What do you think the customer retention rate **(pay and stay)** was as a result? And, do you believe every member told his friends **(referrals)**, about the program?

Strategy & Tactic 5

Generating an Unlimited Amount of Leads for Your Business

Where do your customers come from?

Most people would probably choose advertising as an answer, or referrals, or direct mail campaigns. This may seem true, but it's not really accurate.

Your customers come from leads that have been turned into sales. Each customer goes through a two-step process before they arrive with their wallets open. They have been converted from a member of a target market, to a lead, then to a customer.

So, would it not stand to reason then, that when you advertise or send any marketing material out to your target market, that you're not really trying to generate customers? That instead, you're trying to generate leads.

When you look at your marketing campaign from this perspective, the idea of generating leads as compared to customers seems a lot less daunting. The pressure of closing sales is no longer placed on advertisements or brochures.

From this perspective, the **general purpose of your advertising and marketing efforts is then to generate leads from qualified customers.** Seems easy enough, doesn't it?

Where Are Your Leads Coming From?

If I asked you to tell me the top three ways you generate new sales leads, what would you say?

- ✓ Advertising?
- ✓ Word of mouth?
- ✓ Networking?
- ✓ ...don't know?

The first step toward increasing your leads is in understanding how many leads you currently get on a regular basis, as well as where they come from. Otherwise, how will you know when you're getting more phone calls or walk-in customers?

If you don't know where your leads come from, start *today*. Start asking every customer that comes through your door, "how did you hear about us?" or "what brought you in today?" Ask every customer that calls where they found your telephone number, or email address. Then, *record the information for at least an entire week.*

When you're finished, take a look at your spreadsheet and write your top three lead generators here:

1. _____

2. _____

3. _____

From Lead to Customer: Conversion Rates

Leads mean nothing to your business unless you convert them into customers. You could get hundreds of leads from a single advertisement, but unless those leads result in purchases, it's been a largely unsuccessful (and costly) campaign.

The ratio of leads (potential customers) to transactions (actual customers) is called your conversion rate. Simply divide the number of customers who actually purchased something by the number of customers who inquired about your product or service, and multiply by 100.

 # transactions / # leads x 100 = % conversion rate

If, in a given week, I have 879 customers come in or contact my business, and 143 of them purchase, the formula would look like this:

[143 (customers) / 879 (leads)] x 100 = 16.25% conversion rate

What's Your Conversion Rate?

Based on the formula above, you can see that the higher your conversion rate, the more profitable the business.

Your next step is to determine your own current conversion rate. Add up the number of leads you sourced in the last section, and divide that number into the total transactions that took place in the same week.

Write your conversion rate here: _____.

Quality (or Qualified) Leads

Based on our review of conversion rates, we can see that the number of leads you generate means nothing unless those leads are being converted into customers.

So what affects your ability (and the ability of your team) to turn leads into customers? Do you need to improve your scripts? Your product or service? Find a more competitive edge in the marketplace?

Maybe…but the first steps toward increasing conversion rates is to evaluate the leads you are currently generating, and make sure those leads are the right ones.

What are Quality Leads?

Potential customers are potential customers, right? Anyone who walks into your store or picks up the phone to call your business could be convinced to purchase from you, right? Not necessarily, but this is a common assumption most business owners make.

Quality leads are the people who are the most likely to buy your product or service. They are the qualified buyers who comprise your target market. Anyone might walk in off the street to browse a furniture store – regardless of whether or not they are in the market for a new couch or bed frame. This lead is solely interested in browsing, and is not likely to be converted to a customer.

A quality lead would be someone looking for a new kitchen table, and who specifically drove to that same furniture because a friend had raved about the service they received that month. **These are the kinds of leads you need to focus on generating.**

How Do You Get Quality Leads?

✓ **Know your target market:** Get a handle on who your customers are – the people who are most likely to buy your product or service. Know their age, sex, income, and purchase motivations. From that information you can determine how best to reach your specific audience.

✓ **Focus on the 80/20 rule:** A common statistic in business is that 80% of your revenue comes from 20% of your customers. These are your star clients, or your ideal clients. These are the clients you should focus your efforts on recruiting. This is the easiest way to grow your business and your income.

✓ **Get specific:** Focus not only on who you want to attract, but how you're going to attract them. If you're trying to generate leads from a specific market segment, craft a unique offer to get their attention.

✓ **Be proactive:** Once you've generated a slew of leads, make sure you have the resources to follow up on them. Be diligent and aggressive, and follow up in a timely manner. You've done the work to get them, now reel them in.

Get More Leads from Your Existing Strategies

Increasing your lead generation doesn't necessarily mean diving in and implementing an expensive array of new marketing strategies. Marketing and customer outreach for the purpose of lead generation can be inexpensive, and bring a high return on investment.

You are likely already implementing many of these strategies. With a little tweaking or refinement, you can easily double your leads, and ensure they are more qualified.

Here are some popular ways to generate quality leads:

Direct Mail to Your Ideal Customers

Direct mail is one of the fastest and most effective ways to generate leads that will build your business. It's a simple strategy – in fact, you're probably already reaching out to potential clients through direct mail letters with enticing offers.

The secret to doubling your results is to craft your direct mail campaigns specifically for a highly targeted audience of your *ideal* customers.

Your ideal customers are the people who will buy the most of your products or services. They are the customers who will buy from you over and over again, and refer your business to their friends. They are the group of 20% of your clients who make up 80% of your revenue.

Identify your ideal customers

Who are your ideal customers? What is their age, sex, income, location and purchase motivation? Where do they live? How do they spend their money? Be as specific as possible.

Once you have identified who your ideal customers are, you can begin to determine how you can go about reaching them. Will you mail to households or apartment buildings? Families or retirees? Direct mail lists are available for purchase from a wide range of companies, and can be segregated into a variety of demographic and sociographic categories.

Craft a special offer

Create an offer that's too good to refuse – not for your entire target market, but for your ideal customer. How can you cater to their unique needs and wants? What will be irresistible for them?

Example: if you operate a furniture store, your target market is a broad range of people. However, if you are targeting young families, your offer will be much different than one you may craft for empty-nesters.

Court them for their business

Don't stop at a single mail-out. Sometimes people will throw your letter away two or three times before they are motivated to act. Treat your direct mail campaign like a courtship, and understand that it will happen over time.

First send a letter introducing yourself, and your irresistible offer. Then follow up on a monthly basis with additional letters, newsletters, offers, or flyers. Repetition and reinforcement of your presence is how your customer will go from saying, "who is this company" to "I buy from this company."

Advertise for lead generation

Statistics show that nearly 50% of all purchase decisions are motivated by advertising. It can also be a relatively cost effective way of generating leads.

We've already discussed the importance of ensuring your advertisements are purpose-focused. The general purpose of most advertisements is to increase sales – which starts with leads. However ads that are created solely for lead generation – that is, to get the customers to pick up the phone or walk in the store – are a category of their own.

Lead generation ads are simply designed and create a sense of curiosity or mystery. Often, they feature an almost unbelievable offer. Their purpose is not to convince the customer to buy, but to contact the business for more information.

As always, when you are targeting your ideal audience, you'll need to ensure that your ads are placed prominently in publications your audience reads. This doesn't mean you have to fork over the cash for expensive display ads. Inexpensive advertising in e-mail newsletters, classifieds, and the yellow pages are very effective for lead generation.

Here are some tips for lead generation advertising:

Leverage low-cost advertising

Place ads in the yellow pages, classifieds section, e-mail newsletters, and online. If your target audience is technology savvy, consider new forms of advertising like Facebook and Google AdWords.

Spark curiosity

Don't give them all the information they need to make a decision. Ask them to contact you for the full story, or the complete details of the seemingly outrageous offer.

Grab them with a killer headline

Like all advertising, a compelling headline is essential. Focus on the greatest benefits to the customer, or feature an unbelievable offer.

Referrals and host beneficiary relationships

A referral system is one of the most profitable systems you can create in your business. The beauty is once it's set up, it often runs itself.

Customers that come to you through referrals are often your "ideal customers." They are already trusting and willing to buy. This is one of the most cost-effective methods of generating new business, and is often the most profitable. These referral clients will buy more, faster, and refer further business to your company.

Referrals naturally happen without much effort for reputable businesses, but with a proactive referral strategy you'll certainly double or triple your referrals. Sometimes, you just need to ask!

Here are some easy strategies you can begin to implement today:

Referral incentives

Give your customers a reason to refer business to you. Reward them with discounts, gifts, or free service in exchange for a successful referral.

Referral program

Offer new customers a free product or service to get them in the door. Then, at the end of the transaction, give them three more 'coupons' for the same free product or service that they can give to their friends. Do the same with their friends. This ongoing program will bring you more business than you can imagine.

Host-beneficiary relationships

Forge alliances with non-competitive companies who target your ideal customers. Create cross-promotion and cross-referral direct mail campaigns that benefit both businesses.

Lead Management Systems

Once your lead generation strategies are in place, you'll also need a system to manage incoming inquiries. You'll need to ensure you receive enough information from each lead to follow up on at a later date. You'll also need to create a system to organize that information, and track the lead as it is converted into a sale.

Gathering Information from Your Leads

Here is a list of information you should gather from your leads. This list can be customized to the needs of your business, and the type of information you can realistically ask for from your potential customers.

- ✔ Company Name
- ✔ Name of Contact
- ✔ Alternate Contact Person
- ✔ Mailing Address
- ✔ Phone Number
- ✔ Fax Number
- ✔ Cell Phone
- ✔ Email Address
- ✔ Website Address
- ✔ Product of Interest
- ✔ Other Competitors Engagement

Lead List Management Methods:

Once you have gathered information from your lead, you'll need a system to organize their information and keep a detailed contact history.

The simplest way to do this is with a database program, but you can also use a variety of hard copy methods.

Electronic Database Programs

✓ High level of organization available
✓ Unlimited space for notes and record-keeping
✓ Data-entry required
✓ Examples include: MS Outlook, MS Excel, Maximizer
✓ Customer Relationship Management Software

Index Cards

✓ Variety of sizes: 3x5, 4x6 or 5x8
✓ Basic contact information on one side
✓ Notes on the other side
✓ Easy to organize and sort

Rolodex System

✓ Maintain more contacts than index card system
✓ Easily organized and compact

- ✓ Basic contact information on one side
- ✓ Notes on the other side
- ✓ Can keep phone conversation and purchase details

Notebook

- ✓ Best if leads are managed by a single person
- ✓ Lots of room for notes
- ✓ Inexpensive
- ✓ Difficult to re-organize
- ✓ Best for smaller lists

Business Card Organizer

- ✓ Best for small lists – under 100
- ✓ Limited space for notes
- ✓ No data entry required
- ✓ Rolodex-style, or clear binder pages

Ron's Journal No. 5:

After completing the strategy and tactics in Chapter 1, I created with the client in the examples below, the tactic of creating a special offer as described in this chapter. It was part of every marketing piece and sales presentation.

A women's clinic client in Texas saw its non-critical care patients fall off because it was taking 2 hours to be seen. They offered a 30 minute guarantee unless a grave emergency was taking place. The community responded and **the non-critical patient load almost doubled**.

A builder / developer client in Utah offers to cover all the development costs if they go over budget. Customers don't pay for cost overruns. That builder is **the only one in the market making that offer**. Guess who gets the business?

An equipment company client in South Carolina offers their customers a one week no questions asked 100% refund. 4 customers in 6 six years did so, but **had a 200% growth in that same time period**. The returned equipment was sold right away, with the same guarantee.

A car dealer client in Nebraska **increased their market share by 90%** thru offering a 14 day 100% no questions asked, money back program. A few did return the car (new or used), but the majority wanted to upgrade to a more expensive model, where they earned a larger profit margin.
Which tactic from this chapter will you execute?

Strategy & Tactic 6

Creating Effective Marketing Material

Your marketing collateral gets sent out in the world to do one thing: act as an ambassador for your product or service, in place of *you*. This may seem like a big job for a piece of paper, but it's a helpful way to think about the materials you create.

When you meet with a potential or existing client, you do a number of things. You make sure you are well prepared with all the information the customer could need. You dress in clothing that is appropriate. You anticipate their needs, and offer a solution to their problems. You may also cater to how they best like to receive information.

Chances are you wouldn't meet with clients just for the sake of meeting with a client – say, for instance, to show off your new suit. Likewise, you shouldn't create and distribute collateral that is non-essential.

We all know that the biggest challenge for small businesses is the limited number of zeros attached to their marketing budget. Marketing materials can be expensive, and a single, well-produced piece has the ability to devour the entire budget. Given that billion-dollar marketing campaigns fail every day, how can you be sure to make the most of, and be successful with, the dollars you're working within?

The answer? Limit yourself to only the essential items for your individual business, and produce them *well* with the resources you have.

Your Essential Marketing Materials

The easiest way to throw away your marketing budget is to create and produce marketing materials *you don't need*. Since many pieces of collateral are paper-based, this not only leaves you with boxes of extra (outdated) materials, but also takes a huge toll on the environment.

Take some time to determine what marketing materials you do need, and stick to your list. It's easy to want to "keep up with the Joneses" when your competition comes out with a new piece, but remember your focus should be on attracting and retaining a customer base, not matching the competition item for item.

Know your target market: Make sure you have a solid understanding of your customer base. From that knowledge, you can easily determine what the best way is to reach out and communicate with them. Are they a paper-based or techno savvy client group? Do they appreciate being contacted by email or mail? Are they impressed by flashy design, or simple pieces? *How* you communicate is often just as or more important than *what* you communicate.

Pay attention to costs: Do you really need a die-cut business card? Does your flyer absolutely require ink to the edges? Unique touches to marketing collateral can grab a customer's attention, but they can also dramatically increase the cost of production. Keep an eye out during the design process and make strategic choices about graphic elements.

Make mistakes – in small batches: Not sure if that flyer is going to do the trick? Testing out a limited time offer? Small production runs may cost a little more, but you'll avoid collecting boxes of unusable materials. Or, try a split run with type versions of the same piece and see what works best.

Keep the environment in mind: Environmental responsibility is on everyone's mind these days – including your customers. Always question if a particular marketing item can be produced in electronic format. Consider eliminating plastic bags in exchange for cloth ones, printed with your logo; print everything double-sided; send electronic newsletters; use your website to communicate; and, use recycled paper and envelopes when you can.

Brainstorm your wish list: Create a list of desired marketing materials, and ignore expenses, clients, or any other constraint. Then, beside each item, indicate realistically if it is a needed, wanted, not needed, or electronic item. The next page includes a checklist to get you started. Once you have finished, re-write your list in priority order. This will keep you focused on the essentials only.

Marketing Materials Checklist

Item	Need	Want	Don't Need	Electronic
Logo				
Business Cards				
Brochure				
Website				
Newsletter				
Catalogue				
Advertisements				
Flyers				
Fridge Magnet				
Branded Swag (pens, etc.)				
Employee Clothing				
Product Labels				
Signage				
Internal Templates (Fax Cover, Memo, etc.)				
Email Signature				
Blog				
Letterhead + Envelopes				
Thank You Cards				
Notepads				
Seasonal Gifts				
Company Profile				

Headlines and Sub headlines

If your headlines were all a potential customer read, how do you think your marketing materials would fare? Headlines need to be bold, dramatic, shocking and absolutely answer the questions "What's in it for me?" or, "Why should I care?"

Headlines (and sub headlines) are vital in today's market because we are bombarded with so much information that we scan everything. Readers are skimming your materials to find out why they should bother paying attention to your product or service. Hit their hot buttons, and tell them why they should care, in your headlines!

Remember that headlines and sub headlines are not just for advertisements. They work wonders in newsletters, sales letters, brochures and websites, and can be incorporated into all of your essential marketing materials.

Design

The cost of professional design can eat up the majority of your marketing budget in a hurry. However, the cost of distributing materials that look and feel unprofessional can often be much higher. The key is to find the middle ground.

Unless you have design or desktop publishing experience – or even if you do – your time is probably not best spent designing your own marketing materials. Depending on the size of your business and your graphic needs (i.e., Do you need frequent photography of your products?) there are a number of options you can choose from:

1. **Hire a design agency:** This is no doubt the most costly of your options. However, if you have a number of items to be designed, you may be able to get a package rate. Another option is to have the design agency create a logo and stationery package for you, then create a "how-to" guide for use of the logo, fonts, and other graphic elements in the rest of your marketing materials.

2. **Hire a freelance designer:** For most small businesses, the benefits of using a freelance designer (aside from cost savings) are convenience and trust. If you are lucky enough to find one you work well with, work hard to establish a seamless working relationship and you'll never worry about the design of your marketing materials again. Ask colleagues for recommendations of local designers, or post an ad on craigslist.

3. **Hire a part-time design employee:** Need to hire someone part-time for a task around the office or shop? Consider recruiting someone with design skills and hiring them for full-time work. This could include graphic design students or someone with an interest (and talent) in the field.

Whichever option you choose – or if you choose to design your materials yourself, the two most important things to remember about design are:

1. **Keep it consistent.** Your marketing materials must be consistent, or your customers will never learn to recognize your brand.

2. **Keep it simple.** Simple, clean design is the most effective way of communicating. Use "wow" pieces sparingly.

Guidelines for the Top 10 Marketing Materials

Logo

Use design resources: If you are going to spend any money on outside design help, this is the time to do it. Your logo is the visual representation of your product or service, and appears on everything that relates to your business. This is the core of your brand image, and needs to be done right the first time.

Remember the purpose: The logo needs to be a unique reflection of your business, your business values, and the industry you work in. Before you commit to your logo, make sure to give careful consideration to color choice, image selection and image recognition – as well as the logos that already exist in the marketplace. Test it out on your family and friends for an outside opinion and use their feedback.

Don't get too complicated: Can it be produced (and seen clearly) in black and white? In a single color? With your company name? Too often businesses design their own logos that include a complex assortment of photos, words, and solid design elements. These do not photocopy well, and can't be clearly read at a small scale. Keep your logo design down to a graphic image and the name of your business.

Business cards

Cover the basics: A business card needs to communicate your basic contact information to potential clients, including who you are and *what your business does*. Make sure you've covered the basics and made it easy for them to be in touch.

- ✓ Name
- ✓ Title
- ✓ Company Name
- ✓ Company Slogan / Description
- ✓ Phone Number
- ✓ Email Address
- ✓ Fax Number
- ✓ Address
- ✓ Cell Number (if applicable)
- ✓ Website

Make it memorable and be creative: Choose interesting shapes, die-cuts, orientation (vertical vs. horizontal), bright colors, and unique materials (wood, plastic, magnet, aluminum or foam). You don't have to go crazy or spend lots of money to do this – simple, clever twists on basic design make an impact. Just keep it relevant to your product or service.

Give them a reason to keep it: What is going to keep them from throwing it out, or filing it in a 3" binder of other cards? Make the card worth keeping by adding something useful to the backside.

For example, coffee shops put frequent buyer incentives on the backside of their cards, encouraging customers to keep them in their wallets. Other examples include pick-up schedules, reminders, calendars, testimonials, or coupons.

Produce a high quality card: Use at least 100lb card stock, and print in color. Choose clear, easy to read fonts that aren't any smaller than 9pt.

Letterhead

Ensure a professional quality: Letterhead that is simple, clean, and well produced allows the reader to focus on the important part: the content. Have your letterhead professionally printed on 32lb paper, or choose a textured stock. Show that you are invested in the professionalism of your company.

Pay attention to design choices: The design of your marketing collateral should reflect your corporate values and the personality of your organization. If you are environmentally conscious, choose recycled paper and write it in small print at the bottom of the page. Letterhead can also be a place for subtle graphic elements, like watermarks, in addition to your logo.

Keep consistent with other materials: Your letterhead is part of your stationery package, and should look and feel the same as the rest of your pieces. For example, if your business cards have been printed with rounded corners, so should your letterhead. Use consistent fonts, colors, and logo placement on your letterhead, business cards, fax cover sheets, and other internal documents to ensure recognition and ease of readability.

Brochures

Cover the basics: Each brochure you produce should include your basic marketing message, USP, and detailed company contact information. Product or service features, and customer benefits should be clearly displayed and described.

Be purpose-focused: Why are you producing this brochure? Are you featuring a new product line? Trying to increase awareness? Introducing your service to a new market? Stay closely connected to the purpose behind your brochure, and ensure that all of the information (and images) in the brochure support that purpose.

Keep it simple: Make sure the design and information organization is clean and easy to navigate. Like advertisements, leaving blank spaces gives the reader a break and makes it easier to narrow in on key messages.

Choose high quality production: If you don't invest in your business, why should anyone else? Produce your brochure on high quality paper, in vivid color, and have it professionally folded. An impressive-looking brochure will travel farther than a homemade one – from one client's hands to another's.

Keep it fresh: If you produce brochures on a regular basis, consider giving each a theme to distinguish the information as new and interesting. Keep the overall look and feel consistent, but play with images and content layout to revitalize the design.

Newsletters

Be in touch: Don't wait until your existing clients walk back into your store. Show them they're important to your business, and keep them updated on new products and services by keeping distributing a personalized newsletter.

Use an online distribution service: Online email marketing tools (CRM tools) have never been easier or cheaper to use, and enable you to personalize your letters without much effort. They will also track for you which clients open their newsletters, and which click through to your website.

Provide information, tell a story: Engage the reader with a short anecdote, or a piece of relevant information. Many people are bombarded by hard-copy and electronic letters on a daily basis, so make sure yours is worthy of their reading time. Include an "expert's corner" or "new product feature" and structure the newsletter like your own business newspaper. Add links to relevant media articles, or special offers.

Choose a frequency you can maintain: Newsletters can be time consuming, so be realistic about how often you promise to distribute them. This depends on your resources, and the needs of your business, but generally once a month to once every three months is a good time frame.

Company (or Corporate) Profile

Your ultimate company brochure: Your company profile includes all pertinent information on your business and your offering, and acts as the base for all other marketing items. These are generally longer pieces – from five to 20 pages in length, allowing you ample room for written and visual content.

Tell your story: The company profile is the place to tell the story of your business. Engage the reader, use anecdotes, and describe how and why your company was created. If you inherited the family business, describe how you're carrying on tradition and instilling new life. If you created your company from scratch with your college roommate let the reader know. These real life details are interesting and establish trust with your potential clients and associates.

Communicate your values: Here you have the space to describe your company's vision, values and approach, or philosophies. Make sure you relate your values to your offering, and keep this section short and succinct.

Explain your offering – features, benefits and all: Just like your brochure, make sure to describe the full features and benefits of your product or service. Sprinkle testimonials throughout the design to back up your statements. This can include your full range of services, or simply an overview of your product types. Use professional images and creative copy to keep readers engaged.

Choose high-quality design and production: Spend time creating a company profile that will last. Then, spend money producing one that will impress. Choose glossy paper, and a high-quality press, and leave the profiles around your store and office for clients to read and admire.

Signage

Get professional advice: Outdoor signage can be a daunting task for anyone who hasn't designed, produced, or otherwise gone through the process. Since signage is influenced by a variety of factors – one of which is your municipal government signage bylaw – you may wish to enlist the help of a professional (a signage designer or printer) to guide you through the process and avoid costly errors.

Make it visible: All of your outdoor signage should be easily seen from the street, or within the plaza or complex you are located in. In some cases, you may need more than one sign to do this. Keep in mind how your sign will look at night, as well as during the day, as your company logo and phone number or website needs to be visible at all times.

Make it distinct: When it comes to signage, you can get really creative with materials, lights, and colors. While you need to maintain logo, color, and font consistency, you can add other graphic elements that may not work on the rest of your collateral, including 3D elements and window treatments. Make it memorable.

Remember your indoor signage: Every business needs indoor signage to continually remind customers where they are. This includes section signage, product signage, way finding systems, and promotion announcements. If your business is located in an office, consider signage with your logo and company name above the reception area. Again, keep this signage consistent with the rest of your company materials, and you will be contributing to brand recognition.

Advertisements + Flyers

Place ads strategically: Once you have determined who your target market is, you need to focus on advertising in the publications they are most likely to read, and distributing flyers in places they are most likely to be. Spend ad dollars strategically, and don't spend them all at once. Take time to test what publications work, and which don't by measuring the response from each placement. And, when you place ads, request placement that is well-forward and in the top right hand corner.

Grab their attention: You have less than half a second to grab the attention of your audience with print advertising, so use it wisely. Spend the bulk of your time crafting the headline and choosing compelling images.

Keep their attention: If you caught their attention, you have another two seconds to keep it. Use subheadings to further entice them to read on for the details of your product or service offer.

Tell them why they should buy: Always include your marketing message or USP in your advertising. Describe the features and benefits of your product or service, but focus on the benefits that will trigger an emotional response from your target audience – love, money, luxury, convenience, and security.

Tell them how they can buy: Include a call to action beside your contact information, and include your phone number, website address, and business address (if applicable). You may wish to include a scarcity or urgency offer to compel your readers to act fast.

Know the importance of white space: If you try to cram too much information into your ad or flyer, your readers will skip it. Clean, clear, easy to read ads and one-page flyers with succinct messages are most effective.

Website

Be purpose-focused: Like your brochure, your website can serve a number of purposes. To be effective, you need to narrow in on the specific purpose when designing the content structure of the pages. Who is your audience? What do you want them to leave the site knowing? What do you want the site to make them do? Visit your store? Buy your offering? Pick up the phone? Make sure you are clear on this point before you start.

Make the address easy to remember (and find!): A website address that is too long or too complicated will not get remembered, or found. Do a search for available website addresses that relate to your business or marketing message, and try to secure a site with a .com ending. If your company name is taken, use your USP or guarantee instead.

Focus on content: The overall structure of how you organize the content on your site is like the foundation of your house. You can change the paint color, and the furniture, but the foundation is more or less there for good. Before you work with a designer and create the visual fabric of your website, focus on creating solid copy that is clearly organized. Put together a map of your structure, starting with your homepage and subpages, and allocating specific content to each page.

Revitalize regularly: Your company is always changing, and so should your website. This is an important (and relatively inexpensive) way to communicate your company news and achievements, and most likely the easiest accessed source of information. Have areas for easy content updates – like a "news" section – and make sure sections like "employees" and "services" are kept up to date. For larger updates, go back to your purpose and website map, and make sure the content changes still support the original intent of the website.

Organize for intuition: Make key information easy to access – especially your contact information. You can quickly tell if a website is easy to navigate, because the information you are looking for appears in a natural order. For example, when visiting a restaurant website, a link to the reservations page is provided on the menu page. While you're putting together your website map, do some research online and investigate what does and doesn't work. A good rule of thumb is to ensure it takes no more than three clicks to access a page. Bury content too deep, and your audience will get frustrated and leave.

Keep consistent with marketing materials: Your website is an extension of your marketing campaign, and should be treated as such. Use consistent logo placements, fonts, colors and images so that all elements of your collateral are unified. Likewise with marketing campaigns. If you are running a new promotion, or featuring a new item in an advertisement, include that information on your website. Customers responding to the ad will be reinforced, and customers who did not see the ad will be aware of the offer.

Measure your results: Your website is a piece of your marketing collateral, just like brochures and advertisements, and should be evaluated for effectiveness on a regular basis. Easy website analysis tools, like Google Analytics, will show you which pages your audience is viewing, how long they're staying on each page, and where and when they leave the site. That is powerful information when it comes to structuring content, and choosing which page to put your most important messages.

Ron's Journal No. 6:

A client in Minnesota originally hired me for what is known as an 'Organizational Development' project. The company had no operational structure, assigned responsibility or accountability **and it showed up on the bottom line**.

Soon it became obvious that **the company also had a serious marketing problem.** Everything from their logo, business cards, website, catalogues, to the way the sales staff and delivery drivers dressed, was a hodgepodge. I discovered that everything was designed by different employees who claimed that they had some computer design skills. Big Mistake!

I focused on copywriting. Note I did not say graphic design. Generally, designers are not marketers and only a marketing expert can direct a graphic designer. I worked on the copywriting, creating a unified message, coordinating colors and so on throughout all of their marketing materials as list in this chapter.

We then created a direct mail piece to penetrate new customers. **Direct mail, even today, is still number one.** It's just one of the many marketing material tactics discussed in this chapter, but nowhere can you make a more powerful case, reach customers you'd never get on the phone, make a perfect presentation, get attention, and motivate interest and action prior to face to face contact.

Strategy & Tactic 7

How to Use Advertising for Immediate Profits

Why do you advertise?

Seems like a silly question, doesn't it? Placing ads in newspapers and on the radio seems like a no-brainer way of growing or maintaining your business. You let a group of people know where your business is and what you sell, and you'll always have customers dropping by, right?

Sure, it's a little more complicated than that. There's your powerful offer, your strong guarantee, the placement of your headline, and how you structure your body copy.

But what I'm really trying to drill down to is *why* you chose to place *that* ad. What is the specific purpose for each advertisement you send out into the world? **'Direct Response Advertising', is the only purpose.**

Without a solid purpose – or strategy – behind each and every advertisement, it is impossible to measure what is and is not working. If you placed an ad offering 2 for 1 shampoo one week, and sales for conditioner skyrocketed, would you consider your ad successful?

Absolutely not! Sales might have gone up, but the reason you placed the ad was to speed sales on shampoo, which didn't happen.

The point is that each and every advertising dollar should be spent with purpose, focused on a desired outcome and relevant to the big picture. Advertising is expensive! What's the point, unless you're making your money back and then some?

Types of Advertising

There are endless options when it comes to choosing which media to place your advertisements with. The media is a broad and complicated industry, with highly segmented readership.

This can help and hurt your advertising efforts. You have access to highly targeted audiences, but you also may spend a great deal of money on expensive advertising that your target market doesn't go near.

Here are the major types of media advertising:

Print

Print is the most common form of advertising. Ad production is relatively easy and straightforward, and placement is less expensive than broadcast advertising. We'll be focusing on this form of advertising in detail later in the chapter.

Types of print media:

Newspapers – daily and weekly
Magazines
Trade Journals
Newsletters

Radio

Radio advertising reaches a broad audience within a geographic area. This form of advertising can be highly profitable for some businesses, and utterly useless for others. Always consider if there is a simpler, cheaper way of getting your message to your target audience.

Key points to consider for radio advertising:

Use of sounds, voices, tones
Length
Gaining listener's attention
Call to action

Television

Television advertising is largely out of reach for most small business budgets. Creating, developing, and producing TV spots is a costly endeavor and does not always generate an acceptable return on investment?

This form of advertising generally reaches a broad audience, depending on the timeslot the ad spot airs. Typically, the most expensive airspace is during the region's most popular 6 o'clock news program, or prime time (6pm to 10pm) television line-up.

There are some cost-effective alternatives to TV advertising that you can implement online. You could create a promotional video for your company, and post it on your website and YouTube, or Facebook, or play it in your store. Be creative with your ad budget when it comes to broadcast media.

Online

Online advertising has emerged as an effective tool for your marketing efforts. Internet usage has dramatically increased, and usage patterns have become easier to identify. This form of advertising also allows you to reach a highly qualified audience with minimal investment in ad creation.

Places to advertise online:

Facebook, Twitter, et. al. social media
Google AdWords
Online media (online newspapers and broadcast stations)
Craigslist
Banner ads on complementary websites

Classified

Classified advertising is one of the most highly targeted and cost-effective choices you can make in your overall strategy. People who read classifieds have typically made a decision to buy something, and are looking for places to do so. This is also a great way to test your headlines, offer, and guarantee before you invest in higher-priced advertising.

Classified ad types:

> Daily and weekly newspapers
> Online
> Trade journals

Specific tips for effective classified ads:

✓ Pick a format for your ad within the specifications of the publication. Will it look like a print display ad? A semi-display ad? A classic line ad? This will affect how you structure your message.

✓ Choose the category – or two – that best fit with what you have to offer. If two apply, place an ad in both and measure which category generated more leads.

✓ Grab the attention of your reader with a killer headline, and then list benefits, make an irresistible offer, and offer a strong guarantee. Keep the layout simple and ensure the font size is easy to read.

✓ Notice how other companies are creating their ads, and do something to stand out. The classifieds page is typically cluttered and full of text, so you will need to distinguish your business in some way.

✓ Use standard abbreviations when creating line ads to maintain consistency. Ask the ad department for a list of abbreviations they typically use.

Niche

Niche advertising can take any of the forms discussed above. The advantage of niche advertising is the super segmentation of each outlet's audience. Typically, there is a very small market in each niche, and a single publication that caters to it. This is very effective for companies who have no need for broad market advertising in traditional or mainstream publications.

Types of niche advertising:

Trade journals
Alternative media
Online blogs
Internal communications – newsletters, etc.

Your Advertising Strategy

Develop a strategy that is purpose driven.

Know exactly why you are choosing advertising, as well as the objective of each and every ad. Compare the benefits of advertising to other promotional strategies like media relations, direct mail, referral strategies and customer loyalty programs.

Some common objectives for advertising strategies include:

✔ Generate qualified leads
✔ Increase sales
✔ Promote new products or services
✔ Position products or services
✔ Increase business awareness
✔ Maintain business awareness
✔ Complement existing promotional strategies

These objectives will dictate where you advertise, how big each of your advertisements is, and how often you advertise in each outlet.

Find your target audience: Before you do *anything*, get a solid handle on who your target market is, and each of the segments within it. Think about demographic factors like age, sex, location and occupation, as well as behavioral factors like spending motivations and habits.

The composition of your target audience will be the deciding factor when choosing which media to advertise with, and what to say in each of the advertisements.

Decide on a frequency: The frequency of your advertising campaign will depend on a number of factors, including budget, purpose, outlet, results, and timing. You may wish to publish a weekly ad that includes a coupon in your local paper. Or, you may only need to advertise a few times a year, just before your peak seasons.

Establish an advertising schedule for the year, or at least each quarter, and plan each advertisement in advance. This will ensure you are not scrambling to place an ad at the last minute, and that each ad is part of an overall proactive strategy instead of a reactive one.

Choose your outlets: Decide where you are going to advertise and how often in each outlet. You may wish to choose a variety of media to reach several target audiences, or just a large daily newspaper where the most number of people will see it.

It is a good idea when you are starting a new campaign to test its effectiveness in smaller, less expensive publications. Based on the results, you can make changes to the ad and place it in the more expensive outlets.

Remember that although budget is a large factor when deciding on advertising mediums, it is entirely possible to implement a successful ad campaign with minimal cost investment. The key is to make sure that each dollar you spend is carefully thought through – and that your ads are placed in publications that will reach your ideal customers.

Maximize your ad spend with bulk purchases: If you plan to advertise in a specific publication several times in a given time period, you will benefit from a meeting with the sales representative to review your needs. Often, media outlets will offer discounted rates for multiple placements.

Remember that one company may own several media outlets – including TV, radio, and online media. Ask your sales rep for other discount opportunities when advertising within the ownership group.

Remember to test and measure: How will you know if your campaign is successful if you don't test and measure the results? The only true mistake you can make in advertising is neglecting to track and analyze the results each ad generates.

Get in the habit of keeping a copy of each ad, and record all the details of the placement, including publication, cost, date, response rate, and conversion rate. Many publications will mail you a clipping of your advertisement with your account statement, but don't rely on this as a clipping service.

Evaluate the effectiveness of each ad you place, and learn from what isn't working. If you are advertising in several outlets, make sure asking customers where they saw your ad is part of your incoming phone script and sales script. You will need to monitor not only what types of ads work the best, but also where the ads generate the highest response.

Creating Your Advertisement

You don't need to rely on professional copywriting or design assistance when crafting advertisements from your business. Spend your time and resources on what you are saying, ensure the 'how you say it' is clear, clean, and easy to read.

Ad copy

Headlines

✓ Take at least half of the time you spend creating your ad, and focus on the headline. Your headline will be the difference between your ad getting read – or not. Boldface your headlines for impact.

✓ You have about five seconds to grab the reader's attention, so create a headline that sparks curiosity, communicates benefits, or states something unbelievable.

Sub Headlines

✓ The purpose of your sub headline is to elaborate on your headline, and convince the audience to read the body copy. All the rules of headline writing apply. If you did not mention benefits in your headline, do it in your sub headline. Clearly tell the reader what is "in it for them," and get them reading on.

Body Copy

✓ Choose your words wisely – you don't have room for lengthy paragraphs. Use bullet points to convey benefits wherever possible, and keep your sentences short. You typically only have about 45 words to convince the customer to keep reading.

✓ Remember to always include your contact information – phone number and website address at the very least. This seems obvious, but can be forgotten in the design process.

Ad Layout

Size

✓ Choose your ad size based on the purpose of the ad, and the budget you have available. Larger ads are more expensive, but you do need enough space to communicate your key messages to the audience.

✓ If you place regular ads to maintain a presence in the local paper, you likely don't need full pages of space. Alternately, if you are launching a new product or service, or having a blowout sale, you will want to buy more space to increase the potential impact.

Graphics

✔ Graphics should comprise about 25% of your total ad space, and more if you have a small amount of copy. Avoid drawings and clip art. Photographs will generate a better response. Don't underestimate the importance of white space. Give the reader space to "rest" their eyes between headlines and body copy paragraphs.

Font

✔ Choose clean fonts that are easy to read. Times New Roman and Arial are effective, simple choices. If you use two fonts in your advertisement, make sure you do not combine serif and sans serif fonts, and you keep consistency amongst headers and body copy.

✔ Ensure that none of your copy is smaller than 9pt. Your audience won't take the time or spend the effort to read tiny copy.

Ron's Journal No. 7:

A computer builder / install and service company client in St. Louis believed in advertising and bought from every advertising salesperson who said, "You've got to get your name out there". I'm empathetic to that; I made that same mistake in my earliest years of business ownership.

When I asked how they measured their ad response result…'deer in the headlights'.

Regardless of the media listed in this chapter, the best advertising strategy is called, **'Direct Response Advertising'** (DRA). It asks your customer to respond and allows you to track their response.

97% of small businesses cannot afford to think about 'brand building', you'll go broke. DRA does more than get your name out there.

This computer business was overstocked with hard-drives, RAM and other upgrade type components. So, we created an advertising strategy and the best media to reach their target customer.

The DRA media tactics we used comprised of these 3 crucial elements:

1. An attention grabbing headline

2. An irresistible offer, and …

3. A deadline. Deadlines force action.

The campaign was not the usual 'inventory reduction sale', nobody believes that anymore. It was unusual, different and action oriented, creating many thousands of dollars in additional revenue and a long list of new customers.

Strategy & Tactic 8

How to Double your Referrals

What if I told you that you could put an inexpensive system in place that would effectively allow your business to grow itself?

For most business owners, a large part of their customer base is comprised of referral customers. These people found out about the company's products or services from the recommendation of a friend or colleague who had a positive experience purchasing from that company.

If your business benefits from referral customers, you will find that these customers arrive ready to buy from you, and tend to buy more often. They also tend to be highly loyal to your product or service.

Seems like great customers to have, don't they?

Referral customers cost less to acquire. Compared to the leads you generate from advertising, direct mail campaigns, and other marketing initiatives, referral customers come to you already qualified and already trusting in the quality of your offering and the respectability of your staff.

With a little effort, and the creation of a formalized system – or strategy – you can not only continue to enjoy referral business, but easily double the number of referral customers that walk through your door. All of this is possible for a minimal investment of time and resources.

Is Your Business a Referral Business?

Referral based businesses benefit from a stream of qualified customers who arrive at their doorstep ready to spend. These businesses put less focus on advertising to generate new leads, and more focus on serving and communicating with their existing customers.

Generally speaking, a referral program can generate outstanding results for nearly any business. Since most referrals do not require any effort, the addition of a strategy and a program will often double or triple the number of qualified referrals that come through a business door.

There are, however, a few types of businesses that will not benefit from a formalized referral strategy. These are businesses with low price points – like fast food restaurants and drugstores. Their customer base is large already, and their efforts would be best spent on increasing the average sale.

A referral program can:

✓ **Save you time:** Referral strategies – once established – don't require much management or time investment.

✓ **Deliver more qualified customers:** Your customer arrives with an assumption of trust, and willing to purchase.

✓ **Improve your reputation:** Your customer's networks likely overlap, and create potential for a single customer to be referred by two people. This encourages the perception that your business is "the place to go."

✓ **Speed the sales process:** You will have existing common ground and a reputation with the referred customer.

✓ **Increase your profit:** You will spend less time and money generating leads, and more time serving customers who have their wallets open.

The Cost of Your Customers

As we discussed in the "Repeat Business" section, you don't "get" customers, you *buy* them. The money you spend on advertising, direct mail, and other promotions ideally results in potential customers walking through your doors.

For example, if you placed an ad for $200, and 20 people make a purchase in response to that ad, you would have paid $10 for each customer.

Referral customers cost you next to nothing. Your existing customer does the work of selling your business to their friend or associate, and you benefit from the sale. Aside from the cost of any referral incentives or coupon production, there is no cost involved at all.

Referral customers cost less and require less time investment than any other customer. That means you can spend that time making them a loyal customer, or a devoted fan.

Groom Your Customers

Referral strategies can allow you to groom your customer base. As we have previously discussed, 80% of your revenue comes from 20% of your customers – these are your ideal customers.

These are also the people you have established as your target market, and are the people you cater your marketing and advertising efforts toward.

You also have a group of customers who make up 80% of your headaches. These are the people who complain the most and spend the least.

Use your referral strategy to get more of your *ideal* customers. Spend more time servicing your ideal customers – do everything you can to make them happy – and less time on your headache customers. You can even ask your headache customers to shop elsewhere.

Then, focus your referral efforts on your ideal customers. Ask them to refer business to you, and reward them for doing so. Try to avoid referrals from your headache customers – chances are you'll just get another headache.

Referral Sources

Take some time to brainstorm all the people who could potentially refer business to you. Think beyond your business, to your extracurricular activities and personal life. There are endless sources of people who are ready and willing to send potential customers your way.

Here are some ideas to get you started:

Past Relationships

No, not romantic relationships. I'm talking about anyone you have previously had a relationship with, but for one reason or another have fallen out of touch. This includes former colleagues, associates, customers and friends.

Including them in your referral strategy can be as simple as reaching out through the phone or email, and updating them on your latest business initiative or career move. Gently ask at the end of the correspondence to refer anyone who may need your product or service. *They will appreciate that you have attempted to re-establish the relationship.*

Suppliers and Vendors

Your suppliers and vendors can be a great source for referrals, because they presumably deal daily with businesses that are complementary to your own. The opportunities to connect two of their customers in a mutually beneficial relationship are endless. These businesses should be happy to help out - especially if you have been a regular and loyal customer.

Customers

Customers are an obvious source of referrals because they are the people who are dealing with you directly on a regular basis. Often, all you have to do is ask and they will happily provide you with contact information of other interested buyers, or contact those buyers themselves.

Your customers also have a high level of product knowledge when it comes to your business, and are in a great position to really sell the strength of your company. In the Testimonials section, the words of your customers are at least 10 times more powerful than any clever headline or marketing piece you could create.

Employees and Associates

Give your employees and associates a reason to have their friends and families shop at your business with a simple incentive program. These people have the most product knowledge, and are in the best position to sell you to a potential customer.

This is also a way to tap into an endless network of people. Who do your employees and associates know? Who do their friends and friends of friends know? A referral chain that connects to your employees can be a highly powerful one.

Competitors

This doesn't seem so obvious, but it can work. Your direct competitors are clearly not the ideal source for referrals. However, indirect competitors can refer their clients or potential clients to you if they cannot meet those clients' needs themselves.

For example, if you sell high end lighting fixtures, the low-budget lighting store down the street may be able to refer clients to you, and vice versa. You may wish to offer a finder's fee or incentive to establish this arrangement. *The incentive is more cost effective than trying to sell and special order something that you do not sell.*

Your Network

Don't be shy about asking your friends and family members for referrals. Too many people do not provide enough information to their inner circle about what they do or what their business does. This doesn't make sense, since these are the people who should be the most interested!

Take time to explain clearly what your business is all about, and what your point of difference is. Then just ask them if they know anyone who may benefit from what you are offering. You could even provide your friends and family with an incentive – a gift, a meal, or a portion of the sale.

Associations + Special Interest Groups

This is another place you likely have a network of people who have limited knowledge about what you do or what your business does. The advantage here is that you have a group of people with similar belief s and values in the same room. Use it!

The Media

Unless a member of the media is a regular customer of yours, or you are in business to serve the media, this may not seem like an obvious choice either.

The opportunity here is to establish a relationship with an editor or journalist, and position you as an expert in your field or industry. Then, next time they are writing a related story, they can ask to quote you and your opinion. When their audience reads the story, they will perceive your business as the industry leader.

Referral Strategies

A referral strategy is any system you can put in place to generate new leads through existing customers. The ideal way to do this is to **create a system that runs itself!** Here are some ideas for simple strategies you can begin to implement into your business immediately.

Just Ask

This may seem simple and obvious, but it's true. Be open with your customers and associates, and simply ask them if they can refer any of their friends or associates to you. Make it part of doing business with you, and your customers will grow to expect the question. Or, let them know in advance that you'll be asking at a later date.

Remember that this can include potential customers – even if they don't buy from you. The reason they chose not to purchase may have nothing to do with your business; any person who has begun to or actually done business with you can refer to you another person.

Offer Incentives

When you speak to your customers, when you ask them for something, you typically try to answer the question "what's in it for me?" before they ask it.

The same is true when you ask your customers for a referral. Incentive-based referral strategies work wonders, and can easily be implemented as part of a customer loyalty program, or as part of your existing customer relations systems.

Consider offering customers who successfully refer clients to you discounts on products, free products or services, or gifts. Offer incentives relative to the number of referrals, or the success rate of each referral.

This can have a spin off effect, as your referral customers may become motivated to continue the referral chain. They too will be interested in the incentives you have provided, and tell their friends about your business.

Be Proactive

The only way your referral program will work is if you put some effort into it, and maintain some level of ongoing effort.

Here are some ideas:

- ✓ Put a referral card or coupon in every shopping bag that leaves your store
- ✓ Promote gift certificates during peak seasons
- ✓ Offer free information seminars to existing customers, and ask them to bring a friend
- ✓ Host a closed-door sale for your top 20 customers and their friends

Provide a Great Customer Experience / Service

An easy way to encourage referral business is to treat every potential customer with an exemplary customer experience. Since the art of customer service is lost is many communities, people are often impressed by simple added touches and conveniences. That alone will encourage them to refer your business to their network.

Stay in Touch

Make sure you are staying in touch with all of your potential and converted customers. Through newsletters, direct mail, or the Internet, keep your business name at the top of the mind, ahead of the competition.

Even if they have already purchased from you, and may not need to purchase for some time, a newsletter or email can be a simple reminder that your business is out there. If someone in their network is looking for the product or service, it will be more likely that your customer will refer your business over the competition.

Ron's Journal No. 8:

My consulting, speaking and coaching business has existed almost solely on referrals. Why? It is often very difficult for a business owner to admit they need help, let alone being willing to invest in expertise; when so many friends and industry associates offer advice for free.

But when a client refers a colleague to me, after hearing about the success they now have after working with me, that testimonial referral is essentially pre-sold.

A client in the advertising / public relations business in Michigan had a sales staff that focused on the usual sales activity. Besides the non-existent job-costing, planning and scheduling problems with their business that ate away at their profits, **I also discovered that they had no client referral system in place**.

The following tactics from this chapter were executed immediately.

1. Asked existing advertising clients for non-competitive referrals and credited their account with a PR bonus for the referral

2. Asked suppliers of products featured in ads for referrals

3. Held a 'client appreciation' evening mixer, focused on 'bring a friend' and again credited their account with a PR bonus if the friend ended up being a client.

What do you think the sales people focus on now?

Strategy & Tactic 9

Profits through Building a TEAM
(Together Everyone Achieves More)

The people you employ contribute – directly or indirectly – on a daily basis to the strength and vitality of your business. You can't run your business alone, so you rely on their skills and support.

I recommend you read my article; **Hire Too Fast and / or Fire Too Slow,** *Like a Bach Piano Contest?*
http://ronhequet.com/wp-content/uploads/2015/08/Hire.Too_.Fast_.pdf

But your employees are not just the people who arrive at your office every day and exchange effort for a paycheck. Their role is not just to build capacity and sell more or serve more.

Your employees are part of a potentially powerful group of people that you can leverage to put your business on the fast track to success. Your staff is more than the people who work for you. They are actually members of your team – the group of people who are collectively working to achieve the same objective, or reach the same vision.

I say they are more than just employees because their collective, cohesive value is actually much higher than their individual worth.

We all know that more people working on the same task will ensure the task is completed faster. In business, when you have more people working together on the same task, you save time, increase brainpower, and ultimately, **make more money**.

Corporate Culture

Corporate Culture has become a common buzzword when it comes to building a successful business, and rightly so.

Your corporate culture is the environment in which you run your business, and the environment in which your team members work. It is rooted in the vision, mission and beliefs of the organization, and dictates the "kind of office" and "kind of people" that work in that office.

The business owner and senior employees create a positive or negative environment based solely on who they are as people and how they behave as leaders. You simply can't avoid creating some type of corporate culture when you run a business.

I recommend you read my article; **Wally Who?** *Don't Let Anyone Hijack Your Company Culture*
http://ronhequet.com/wp-content/uploads/2015/08/Wally.Who_.pdf
You can, however, avoid creating a negative or unproductive corporate culture. Whether you are just starting out, or seeking to improve your workplace, you do have control over the type of environment in which you run your business.

Like most things in business, this won't happen overnight. However, with a clear idea of where you want to go, and what you want to create, you'll be well on your way to getting there.

Vision

Your company's vision statement should be a bold, clear, short sentence that every single one of your employees knows and understands. It is a roadmap to your idea of success; if you don't know what that looks like, how will you know when you achieve it?

If your goal is to create a highly profitable company – what does highly profitable mean? $1 million in annual sales? $3 million in annual profit?

Do you seek to become the industry leader in sprocket production? How will this be measured? How many sprockets will you have to produce to reach this goal?

The vision statement is a short summary of the long-term objective of the company. What the company will look like, produce, achieve; it is how you know the company is "successful."

Many companies either do not have a vision statement or they keep it a secret from their employees. It is only discussed in board meetings or management meetings. For a team to collectively work toward a goal, they need to know what the big picture objective is. They need to have buy-in in the company's direction, and be communicated with on a regular basis.

Be proud of your vision. Keep it visible for staff – post it on the wall, include it in internal communications, and connect day-to-day activities to it as often as possible.

Sample Vision Statements

Here are some real examples of corporate vision statements:

"At Microsoft, our mission and values are to help people and businesses through the world realize their potential." – Microsoft

"Give every customer a reason to believe…STAPLES Business Depot—That was easy!" – Staples Canada

"To build the largest and most complete Amateur Radio community site on the Internet." – eHam.net

Creating a Vision Statement

The process of creating a vision statement is something that you can work through alone, or in collaboration with your team. It is highly recommended to review the draft vision statement with your employees to ensure they understand and support the goals and objectives of the company.

Keep the following points in mind when crafting your vision statement:

✓ **Think big** – Why did you start or buy this business? What was your dream or purpose in doing so?

✓ **Think long-term** – Vision statements should last five to 10 or even 25 years

✓ **Be specific** – Use numbers, dates, ratings systems and other ways of measuring success

✓ **Be succinct** – Use clear, short, simple sentences that are easy to repeat and remember

Mission

Your mission statement is a general description of how you are going to achieve your vision. This is a longer and more detailed statement that should include what your business is, who your customers are, and how you are different from (better than!) the competition.

Sample Mission Statements

"The Mission of McGill University is the advancement of learning through teaching, scholarship and service to society: by offering to outstanding undergraduate and graduate students the best education available; by carrying out scholarly activities judged to be excellent when measured against the highest international standards; and by providing service to society in those ways for which we are well-suited by virtue of our academic strengths." – McGill University, Montreal, Canada

"Starbucks purchases and roasts high-quality whole bean coffees and sells them along with fresh, rich-brewed, Italian style espresso beverages, a variety of pastries and confections, and coffee-related accessories and equipment -- primarily through its company-operated retail stores. In addition to sales through our company-operated retail stores, Starbucks sells whole bean coffees through a specialty sales group and supermarkets. Additionally, Starbucks produces and sells bottled Frappuccino® coffee drink and a line of premium ice creams through its joint venture partnerships and offers a line of innovative premium teas produced by its wholly owned subsidiary, Tazo Tea Company. The Company's objective is to establish Starbucks as the most recognized and respected brand in the world." – Starbucks

Creating Your Mission Statement:

Here is a recommended process for completing your mission statement:

Step One: List your company's core strengths and weaknesses; what do you do well? What do you need to work on, or avoid doing?

Step Two: Who are your primary customers? Describe the types of customers you serve – both internal and external

Step Three: What do your customers think of your strengths? What strengths are most important to them? Go ahead and ask them if you need to

Step Four: Connect the strength that each customer values with its customer type. Write it in a sentence. Combine any redundancies

Step Five: Organize your sentences in order of importance

Step Six: Combine your sentences into a paragraph or two. Elaborate on points as needed. This is your draft mission statement.

Step Six: Consult with your staff and customers, and ask for their feedback. Do employees support the statement? Can they act on it? Do customers want to do business with a company with this mission statement? Does it make sense?

Step Seven: Incorporate the feedback received, and refine the statement until you are happy with it. Then publish it – everywhere.

Culture or Values Statements

Your culture or values statement is the next step in the process. It describes how you and your staff will go about taking action (your mission statement) to achieve your objective (your vision statement).

Much like every family has their own belief system and way of doing things – from cooking to cleaning to raising kids – every company has their own set of values when it comes to running a business. It reflects the unique personality of the organization.

Sample Culture Statement

Our Culture

* Values-based leadership: Our Credo outlines the values that provide the foundation of how we act as a corporation and as individual employees so that we continue to put the needs of the people we serve first.

* Diversity: It's our individual differences that make us stronger as a whole. We recognize the strength and value that comes when collaborative relationships are built between people of different ages, race, gender, religion, nationality, sexual orientation, physical ability, thinking style, personal backgrounds and all other attributes that make each person unique.

* Innovation: True innovation can only be fostered within a supportive environment that values calculated risk in order to achieve the maximum reward. At Johnson & Johnson Inc., we encourage and reward innovative thinking, innovative solutions and an innovative approach in all that we do.

* Passion: The deep desire to enrich people's lives – by delivering quality products and remarkable experiences that make their lives easier, healthier and more joyful.

* Collaboration: The unwavering belief that great results depend on the ability to create trusting relationships.

* Courage: The fearless pursuit of the unproven, unknown possibility – the willingness to take great risks for the benefit of the greater good.

Creating Your Culture Statement

Involve your team in creating your company's culture or values statement. Generally, this is a point-form document that reflects the beliefs of the company, its employees, and its customers.

It can be helpful to think about the type of people you currently employ, as well as the ones you may wish to employ. What are they like? What are their belief systems? What are their most important values?

Remember that the culture or values statement is usually the longest of the three statements – and that's okay.

Your Team Leaders

The strength of a team lies in the strength of the people who lead it. No group of people is effective without strong leadership, just like no business is effective without a strong owner or management team.

Building a strong team means knowing who your leaders are – both in job description and natural ability.

Understanding the strength of your natural leaders and the skills of your natural followers will allow you to strategically structure your team for maximum effectiveness and efficiency. It will give your insight into who is best suited for management promotions and project management; which team members have the ability to assemble and motivate their peers.

Your leaders need to have a high degree of passion for your product or service, and truly believe in the company's vision. They need to be able to handle a high level of responsibility, and manage a range of people to achieve a common goal.

Your leaders are your team builders. They present new ideas, build consensus, and encourage the involvement of others.

Types of Leaders

Simply speaking, there are four main types, or styles, of leaders. Chances are you've experienced each type at some point in your career.

Type	Description	Ideal Use
Autocratic	Classical or "old-school" approach Manager holds all power and decision-making authority No employee consultation or input Orders are obeyed Rewards/punishment structure	New, untrained employees Detailed orders and instructions are required No other leadership style has been effective Limited time available Department restructuring High production requirements
Bureaucratic	"By the book" approach All is done to specific procedures/policies All tasks outside policies referred to higher management	Routine tasks performed Standards and procedures need to be communicated regularly Safety or training Cash handling Dangerous equipment
Laissez-faire	"Hands-off" approach Employees have almost total freedom Little direction or guidance is provided Employees must make own decisions, set own goals Employees must solve own problems	Highly skilled and experienced employees Employees are highly driven and ambitious Consultants are being managed Employees are trustworthy

Representative	"Participatory approach" Employees part of decision making process Employees well informed Leader has final say, but involves others Collaborative approach Encourages employee development with guidance and assistance from leader Leader recognizes and rewards achievement	Collaborative environment Employee development and growth is the focus Changes or problems affect employees and require their input to create a solution Team building and participation is encouraged

Communication

The only way to build and maintain a strong team is through strong, consistent communication. This is often an overlooked or neglected aspect of business management, and is easily forgotten during periods of high stress or heavy workload.

Avoid letting communication fall on the backburner by creating a regular meeting schedule – and sticking to it. Depending on the size and type of your business, daily, weekly, or monthly team meetings are an important cornerstone of a strong team.

Regularly scheduled team meetings are like Sunday dinners with a busy family. They give you – the owner – a regular forum with your staff to implement company-wide training initiatives, announce results, establish goals and targets, or share new visions or directions. They also give your staff a forum to share feedback and air grievances.

Effective Team Meetings

By now you're probably thinking, 'Sure, I hear some company's team meetings are effective, but we tried them and it didn't work' or 'I held regular team meetings, but after a while, no one showed up.'

There is a difference between team meetings held for the sake of having team meetings, and well prepared team meetings with a purpose. *You need to start holding team meetings with a purpose.*

Establish a Schedule That Everyone Can Commit To

Scheduling is potentially the biggest challenge when trying to set up a team meeting. Often, all of your staff members are busy going in eight different directions to fulfill their roles and operating on dramatically different schedules.

This is one reason why regular team meetings are important. Ad hoc meetings require ad hoc scheduling, and reduce the likelihood that all your team members will be able to attend.

Ask your team to block off one hour each week (or month) for the team meeting in a time slot that is convenient for everyone.

Establish a clear attendance expectation from everyone. This will exclude that time slot from the scheduling of other meetings and avoid conflict.

If you find that a team meeting is not necessary one week, you can always cancel it.

Know Your Purpose

Each team meeting should have a purpose and clear objectives. Is it to educate? Build consensus? Gather feedback?

Once you have established a purpose for a particular meeting, **send an agenda** to your staff confirming the meeting and outlining your objectives. This is a good time to ask if anyone has a subject they would like to discuss at the meeting.

If you find you do not have a clear purpose or objective, ask yourself if a team meeting is the best use of time for that week and consider postponing it to the next regularly scheduled time slot.

Plan Each and Every Minute

The biggest complaint from employees about team meetings is the length. Too often team meetings run out of control, and end up taking three hours instead of one. You will quickly lose team focus and respect for the regular meeting this way. By establishing a clear agenda and staying on topic, you can run an efficient, succinct meeting.

Your detailed agenda should include:

✓ meeting purpose or objective
✓ list of topics and associated speakers
✓ list of decisions that need to be made/agreed to
✓ time allocation for each topic
✓ opportunity for additional topics at the end

Circulate your draft agenda in advance of the meeting, and request input and feedback. When all team members have reviewed and contributed to the agenda, you will increase their level of ownership and buy-in into the process.

Establish the Facilitator

Choose one person to chair the meeting and keep it on track. This is generally the business owner or a senior member of the team with some authority over junior staff and a high level of respect.

It is the responsibility of the facilitator – or chairperson – to create an environment of open dialogue and trust, and to keep the meeting on schedule.

Create a Follow-up Schedule

Assign the task of taking detailed meeting minutes to a team member – or rotate this responsibility on a regular basis. It is important to record what happens in team meetings, just as you would in a client-related business meeting.

In the minutes, establish a system for tracking the action items that arise from decisions made in the meeting. This can be set up as a simple chart:

Decision	Action	Responsibility	Deadline

Make sure that these responsibilities are assigned and agreed upon in the meeting, and clear deadlines are established. Reviewing or following up on this chart can serve as a regular topic during team meetings.

Circulate meeting minutes to all attendees and ask for input or revisions. You may wish to circulate meeting minutes with the agenda for the next team meeting, and gather feedback at the same time.

Motivations and Incentives

A big challenge in team building is coming up with new ways to foster and maintain a high level of motivation. How do you keep teams of people excited and driven to succeed over long periods of time? How do you keep your team motivated to improve their performance, and increase their achievements?

It is important to note that we're not just talking about individuals, but teams of people working together. It is fairly simple to motivate a single person, but an entire team of motivated people will generate significantly higher results.

The key here is to give incentives for individual and team accomplishments. Incentives that reward based on collective achievement require people to work together and motivate each other to succeed.

Before we start talking about monetary and incentive-based rewards, it's important to look at motivational factors that are not incentive-driven.

Room to Work

Employees who feel their managers and supervisors believe and trust in their abilities, are happier and will always perform at a higher level than those who do not. They are motivated to 'prove them right' and feel supported in their efforts.

Micromanagement quickly reduces morale. It is essential that you and your managers clearly express confidence in your team members. You hired them to do a job, perform a role, so you must ensure they have the space to do so.

When you put effective systems in place and establish clear expectations, you create a clear context or boundary system for employees to work within. They understand the decision-making hierarchy, and the general way 'things are done around here.'

Your team should be encouraged to take initiative and to take risks within this context. You have hired your team based on their skills and intellectual capabilities, and thus should be able to trust in their choices and decision making abilities.

Incentives

Incentives are great motivators. An incentive is a reason to perform or act in a certain way. For example, if your team increases sales by 40% by month's end, they will be treated to an expensive dinner.

Incentives need to be specific and have deadlines in order to be effective. In the example above, sales need to increase by 40% by the end of the month in order for the team to receive their dinner. If sales only increase by 30%, or if they increase by 40% at the end of the second month, the team does not earn their reward.

Time-specific incentives increase the sense of urgency, and encourage staff to work harder to achieve the objective. If the incentive is not time-bound, there is no reason to work faster or harder, since staff will assume they will reach their milestone 'eventually'.

Rarity is also a key component of effective incentive-based team building. If the reward is ongoing (i.e., if staff receive an expensive dinner every month sales are over $75,000), then "there's always next time." There is a lesser incentive to push performance to receive the reward. Some team members may care one month, but not the next.

Monetary Incentives

Bonuses and salary increases are a popular way to give your team an incentive to perform. These can include:

- ✓ Commissions
- ✓ Bonuses for completing a challenging project, or hitting a target
- ✓ Rewards for highest producing employee
- ✓ Salary increases based on met targets

It's up to you how you choose to structure your monetary incentives, based on your budget and resources. Remember to ensure that the terms of each incentive are clearly outlined, and that both parties (you and your employee) understand the agreement.

Gift Rewards

Physical, tangible gifts are an inexpensive way to reward your team for achievements and improvement. These rewards show that you have given some level of thought to what they might enjoy or appreciate in exchange for a job well done. They're also a great way to surprise employees.

Here are some ideas:

✓ Spa gift certificates
✓ Books – *consider motivational or business-related topics*
✓ CDs or DVDs
✓ Meals – lunch or breakfast
✓ Other gift certificates – gas, food, meals, local shops
✓ Movie or theatre tickets
✓ Weekend getaway – hotel, meals, etc.
✓ Flowers
✓ Gym memberships

Ron's Journal No. 9:

A client in the meat processing business in Texas hired me because as they said, 'We're so disorganized, that we're running lift trucks into walls'.

The 4 owners believed that if management had designated position descriptions with predetermined function, authorities and assigned responsibilities the organization would operate more efficiently. In part, they were correct, but they did not see the organization through my eyes.

What once was a small building with a handful of employees was now a 100K sq. ft. facility with +/-400 employees and not a team among them. No amount of job descriptions or organizational charts would fix this organization.

If you've read my journal entries in this book, you know that I, in collaboration with the owners, turned this nightmare of an organization into a highly functioning and more profitable company, by applying the principle tactics in this chapter.

1. Defined the company culture

2. Created the Vision, Values and Mission Statements

3. Created 6 person teams in all departments

4. Trained team leaders in leadership, communication and planning

5. Created incentives for productivity and results

Over the next year, this project created an additional 2% to the net operating profit on a multi-million dollar company.

Strategy & Tactic 10

Systemizing Your Business and Developing Effective Processes

One of the biggest mistakes a business owner can make is to create a company that is dependent on the owner's involvement for the success of its daily operations. This is called working **in** your business. You're writing basic sales letters, licking stamps, and guiding staff step-by-step through each task.

There are a number of problems with this approach. One is redundancy. You're paying your staff to carry out tasks that you eventually complete. The second is poor time management. You're spending your day – at your high hourly rate – on tasks as they arise, leaving little room for the tasks you need to be focused on.

However, the biggest issue I have with this approach is that countless intelligent business owners are spending the majority of their time operating their business, instead of *growing* it.

A good test of this is to ask yourself what would happen if you took off to a hot sunny destination for three weeks and left your cell phone, PDA and laptop at home. **Would your business be able to continue operating?**
If you said no, then this chapter is for you.

Systemizing your business is about putting policies and procedures in place to make your business operations run smoother – and more importantly – without your constant involvement. With your newfound free time, **you will be able to focus your efforts on the bigger picture: strategically and tactically growing your business.**

Why Systemize?

For most small business owners, systems simply mean freedom from the day-to-day functioning of their organization. The company runs smoothly, makes a profit, and provides a high level of service – regardless of the owner's involvement.

Systemizing your business is also a healthy way to plan for the future. You're not going to be working forever – what happens when you retire? How will you transition your business to new ownership or management? How will you take that vacation you've been dreaming of?

Businesses that function without their ownership are also highly valuable to investors. Systemizing your business can position it in a favorable light for purchase, and merit a high price tag.

A system is any process, policy, or procedure that consistently achieves the same result, regardless of who is completing the task.
Any task that is performed in your business more than once by different people can be systemized. Ideally, the tasks that are completed on a cyclical basis – daily, weekly, monthly, and quarterly – should be systemized so much so that anyone can perform them.

Systems can take many forms – from manuals and instruction sheets, to signs, banners, and audio or video recordings. They don't have to be elaborate or extensive, just provide enough information in step-by-step form to guide the person performing the task.

NOTE: Any process, procedure, task or duty that is not documented in any of the above mentioned formats, will be performed at the employees discretion.

Benefits of Business Systems

There are unlimited benefits available to you and your business through systemization. The more systems you can successfully implement, the more benefits you'll see.

✓ Better cost management
✓ Improved time management
✓ Clearer expectations of staff
✓ More effective staff training and orientation
✓ Increased productivity (and potentially profits)
✓ Happier customers (consistent service)
✓ Maximized conversion rates
✓ Increased staff respect for your time
✓ Increased level of individual initiative
✓ Greater focus on long-term business growth

Taking Stock of Your Existing Systems

The first step in systemizing your business is taking a long look at the existing systems (if any) in your business. At this point, you can look for any systems that have simply emerged as "the way we do things here."

How does your staff answer the phone? What is the process customers go through when dealing with your business? How are employees hired? Trained? How is performance reviewed and rewarded?

Some of your systems may be highly effective, and not require any changes. Others may be ineffective and require some reworking. If you have previously established some systems, now is a good time to check-in and evaluate how well they are functioning.

Use the following chart to record what systems currently exist in your business.

Existing Systems	
Admin.	
Financials	
Communication	
Customer Relations	
Employees	
Marketing	
Data	

Seven Areas to Systemize

There is no doubt that system creation – especially when none exist to begin with – is a daunting and time-consuming task.

Begin with one area, and move to the other areas as you are ready. Alternately, start with one or two systems within each area, and evaluate how those new systems affect your business. Each business will require its own unique set of systems.

1. Administration

This is an important area of your business to systemize because administrative roles tend to see a high turnover. A series of systems will reduce training time, and keep you from explaining how the phones are to be answered each time a new receptionist joins your team.

Administrative Systems	
Opening and closing procedures	Filing and paper management
Phone greeting	Workflow
Mail processing	Document production
Sending couriers	Inventory management
Office maintenance (watering plants, emptying recycle bins, etc.)	Order processing
	Making orders

2. Financials

This is one area of systems that you will need to keep a close eye on – but that doesn't mean you have to do the work yourself. Financial management systems are everything from tracking credit card purchases to invoicing clients and following up on overdue accounts.

These systems will help to prevent employee theft, and allow you to always have a clear picture of your numbers. It will allow you to control purchasing, and ensure that each decision is signed-off on.

Financial Systems	
Purchasing	Profit / loss statements
Credit card purchase tracking	Invoicing
Accounts payable	Daily cash out
Accounts receivable	Petty cash
Bank deposits	Employee expenses
Cutting checks	Payroll
Tax payments	Commission payments

3. Communications

The area of communication is essential and time consuming for any business. Fax cover letters, sales letters, internal memos, reports, and newsletters are items that need to be created regularly by different people in your organization. Most of the time, these communications aren't much different from one to the next, yet each are created from scratch by a different person. There is a huge opportunity for systemization in this area of your business. Systemized communication ensures consistency and company differentiation.

Communication Systems	
Internal memo template	Newsletter template
Fax cover template	Sales letter template(s)
Letterhead template	Meeting minutes template
Team meeting agenda	Report template
Sending faxes	Internal meetings
Internal emails	Scheduling

4. Customer Relations

Another important area for systemization is customer relations. This includes everything the customer sees or touches in your company, as well as any interaction they might have with you or your staff members.

Establishing a customer relations system will also ensure that new staff members understand how customers are handled in *your* business. It will allow you to maintain a high level of customer service, without constantly reminding staff of your policies. It will also ensure that the success of your customer relations and retention does not hinge on you or any other individual salesperson.

Customer Relations Systems	
Incoming phone call script	Sales process
Outgoing phone call script	Sales script
Customer service standards	Newsletter templates
Customer retention strategy	Ongoing customer communication
Customer communications templates	strategy
	Customer liaison policy

5. Employees

Create systems in your business for hiring, training, and developing your employees. This will establish clear expectations for the employee, and streamline time-consuming activities like recruitment.

Employees with clear expectations who work within clear structures are happier and more productive. They are motivated to achieve 'A' when they know they will receive 'B' if they do. Establishing a clear training manual will also save you and your staff the time and hassle of training each new staff member on the fly.

Employee Systems	
Employee recruitment	Staff uniforms or dress code
Employee retention	Employee training
Incentive and rewards program	Ongoing training and professional
Regular employee reviews	development
Employee feedback structure	Job descriptions and role profiles

6. Marketing

This is likely an area in which you spend a large part of your time. You focus on generating new leads and getting more people to call you or walk through your doors. These efforts can be systemized and delegated to other staff members.

Use the information in this program to create simple systems for your basic promotional efforts. Any one of your staff should be able to pick up a marketing manual and implement a successful direct mail campaign or place a purposeful advertisement.

Marketing Systems

Referral program	Regular advertisements
Customer retention program	Advertisement creation system
Regular promotions	Direct mail system
Marketing calendar	Sales procedures
Enquiries management	Lead management

7. Data

While we like to think we operate a paperless office, often the opposite is true. Your business needs to have clear systems for managing paper and electronic information to ensure that information is protected, easily accessed, and only kept when necessary.

Data management systems help you keep your office organized. Everyone knows where information is to be stored, and how it is to be handled, which prevents big stacks of paper with no place to go.

Ensure that within your data management systems you include a data backup system. That way, if anything happens to you server or computer software, your data – and potentially your business – is protected.

Data Management Systems	
IT Management	Client file system
Data backup	Project file system
Computer repairs	Point of sale system
Electronic information storage	Financial data management

Implementing New Systems

If you completed the exercise earlier in this chapter, you will have a good idea of the systems that are currently in place in your business. The next step is to determine what systems you need to create in your business.

To do this you will need to get a better understanding of the tasks that you and your employees complete on a daily and weekly basis. If you operate a timesheet program, this can be a good source of information. Alternately, ask staff to keep a daily log for a week of all the tasks they contribute to or complete.

Doing so will not only give you valuable insight into their how they spend their time on a daily basis, but also involve them in the systemizing process.

Review all task logs or timesheet records at the end of the week, remove duplicates, and group like tasks together. From here you can categorize the tasks into business areas like the seven listed above, or create your own categories.

Then, you will need to prioritize and plan your system creation and implementation efforts. Choose one from each category, or one category to focus on at a time. The amount you can take on will depend on your business needs, and the staff resources you have available to you for this process.

Remember that system creation is a long-term process – not something that will transform your business overnight. Be patient, and focus on the items that hold the highest priority.

Creating Your Systems

There is a big variety of ways you can create systems for your business – depending on the type of system you need and the type of business you operate. Some systems will be short and simple – i.e., a laminated sign in the kitchen that outlines step-by-step how to make the coffee – while others will be more complex – i.e., your sales scripts or letter templates.

One thing all of your systems have in common is steps. There is a linear process involved from start to finish. Begin by writing out each of the steps involved in completing the task, and provide as much detail as you can.

Then, review your step-by-step guide with the employee(s) who regularly complete the task and gather their feedback. Once you have incorporated their input, decide what format the system needs to be in: manual, laminated instruction sheet, sign, office memo, etc.

Testing Your Systems

Now that you have created a system, you will need to make sure that it works. More specifically, you need to make sure that it works without your involvement.

Implement the new system for an appropriate period of time – a week or month – then ask for input from staff, suppliers and vendors, and customers. Evaluate if it is informative enough for your staff, seamless enough for your suppliers, and whether or not it meets or exceeds your customer's needs.

Take that feedback and revise the system accordingly. You will rarely get the system right the first time – so be patient.

Systems will also need to be evaluated and revised on a regular basis to ensure your business processes are kept up to date. Structure an annual or bi-annual review of systems, and stick to it.

Employee Buy-In

It will be nearly impossible for you to develop effective systems without the involvement and input of your employees. These are the people who will be using the systems, and who are completing the tasks on a regular basis without systems. They have a wealth of knowledge to assist you in this process.

Employees can also draft the systems for you to review and finalize. This will make the systemization process a much faster and more efficient one.

It is also important to note that when you introduce new systems into your company, there may be a natural resistance to the change. People – including your employees – are habitual people who can become set in the way they are used to doing things.

NOTE: You, the owner must impose the final decision as to how your systems are to be executed.

Delegation

The final step to systemizing your business is delegation. What is the point of creating systems unless someone other than you can use them to perform tasks?

This doesn't have to mean completely removing your involvement from the process, but it does mean giving your employees enough freedom to complete the task within the structure of the systems you have spent time and considerable thought creating.

After that, allow yourself the freedom of focusing on the tasks that you most enjoy, and most deserve your time – like creating big picture strategies to grow your business and increase your profits.

Ron's Journal No. 10:

This chapter was placed last for a reason. With my marketing expertise and experience, I can grow your business. But with growth comes really nice problems to have, i.e. more employees, larger facilities, more overhead, etc. Without documented systems, you're asking for trouble.

When arriving at a client facility to perform a 'Business Analysis', one of the many documents I ask for is the 'Employee Policy Manual' and the 'Company Operations Manual'. **I can't ever remember receiving the later** and the former is typically a handbook, which doesn't meet legal or other requirements.

A CNC Milling and Screw Machine business client in Chicago asked for my help to improve productivity and many other issues. They designed and manufactured cutting tools for the aerospace industry. They too did not have an 'Operations Manual' or a formal training program.

They did not formally track what is commonly known as 're-do work', i.e. a part that was not made to specifications that had to be re-worked. I decided to perform a time and motion study on the work flow.
Standing next to a worker at a large machine, I asked, "Who trained you to do this particular part of the job?" He pointed to a man several machines down the line. So, I walked over to him and asked the same question and got the same answer – pointing to yet another worker in the plant.
continued...

continued...

My point here is that the work processes were basically trained via on the job training (OJT). Therefore, how to do something was subject to each workers interpretation, e.g. a lack of consistency and the cause for a lot of 're-do' work. **How do you think that effected productivity costs?**

You may not have a milling plant operation and I don't care if you are a 2 person business or 200. Today's average employment tenure in the U.S. is 3-5 years. Hence, **there will be turn-over in all businesses**.

Remember the game at the fair, 'Whack-a- Mole'? Do you or your employees feel like their whacking at moles? How much training time **(money)**, how many errors **(money)**, how much consistency would be gained **(money)**, how much of your time **(money / stress)** would result if your businesses way of doing things was documented. And I mean 'everything', from scripts on how to use the phone, customer service responses, to how to reconcile and make a bank deposit, et al.

Documenting goals, principles, processes and procedures are for action and decision making for you and your team. This is not a 'feel good' exercise. It is the mandatory foundation for creating tremendous efficiency **(money)**.

continued...

continued...

One of the businesses I owned was a multi-location retail company. I wrote the entire point of sale POS manual, along with all the operating policies and procedures. Literally, **a new employee could open the manual and follow the step by step instructions on how to perform any transaction**; from handling a product return to cleaning the bathroom.

Write it down: The beginning of documentation is where you can drop the ball, not just because this is all new, but because you may still be going from fire to fire, pulling you back into serial mole whacking.

Dedicate the time: If you think this can be done in your 'free' time, you're wrong and that sort of thinking will always give way to the 'crisis du jour'.

How to Summary

1. Make a list of all recurring processes
2. Avoid bureaucracy, random or seldom occurring situations
3. Involve your team to compose and delegate
4. Format each procedure identical in appearance
5. Test every procedure, delegate
6. As the owner, you must sign off to ensure each procedure is congruent

continued...

continued...

Your competition doesn't do it: Frank Zappa 1940-2003, (I was not a fan of the music, but a fan of the person), was one of the most brilliant avant-garde rock artists of the 70's-80's. **He had a system improvement strategy.**

Frank scored (wrote down) each note of every song and demanded 100% performance accuracy. After a concert, while his contemporaries most likely partied, Frank would hold a mandatory attendance post-concert meeting with his band.

Individual players were given a $50 fine for each and every note missed. New band members were quick to challenge Frank's recollection of the score and their performance (older members knew better). Frank had perfect recall of the concert, the missed notes were verified with the concerts audio recording, and the fines stood. Fined band members were likely to rehearse their parts before the next concert...ya think?

Frank Zappa set the bar high and his success is rock music history.

Does this attention to detail seem nitpicky? If so, your challenge is to welcome this level of attention rather than blow it off.

The end result: Less work, more time and yes...**more money!**

I understand that Frank Zappa never used drugs and was a good family man.

Leverage from Marketing Case Studies

The strategies in this program mean absolutely nothing unless you choose to implement them.

The beauty of each of these time-tested strategies is that you can begin implementing them at any time – and start virtually anywhere in the program. There is no need to completely rework your entire marketing campaign or put off making changes until you can make all the changes at once.

This section profiles the success of others who have taken the information in this program and used it to better their businesses.

In each case, it took only a handful of changes to dramatically increase sales and generate higher revenues.

Let their stories motivate you to start working today to better your own business.

Case Study No. 1

Think Coffee News

Business Type: Small Magazine Publisher

Objective: Increase profits with cross selling opportunities, without any time expense.

Strategy: Education

Solution(s): A prominent marketing personality was asked to write a regular column and create a series of workshops. The column and workshops were designed to educate clients on easy-to-implement and cutting-edge marketing initiatives, as well as sell clients a twelve-month program (Starter Program).

Value Added Proposition: The twelve-month program would assist advertising clients on marketing their own business, creating better offers, back end sales, as well as profitable joint-venture opportunities.

Method: Free Series of Marketing Workshops + Newsletter Column

Marketing Materials:

✓ Sales Script to promote Starter Program

✓ Email template

✓ Workshop invitation

Result! A sustainable joint venture and cross selling opportunity was established, and is now worth thousands of dollars in additional revenue per year.

Case Study No. 2

Young Realtor of the Year

Business Type: Independent Contractor

Issue: Need to increase revenues, but has no extra time available after a successful marketing campaign.

Strategy: Intellectual Capital

Solution(s): When other local realtors phone for free advice, he sells them on shadowing him in action for a day. Less successful realtors ride his coattails for a day and are free to take as many notes as they like. Must guarantee they will not impede his ability to work nor talk to his clients at any stage.

Value Added Proposition: A one-hour debrief is included in the session, plus a hand out to ensure the client experienced/noticed most important parts of day. A less successful realtor is educated, and the young realtor is positioned as an expert through this mentorship program.

Method: Regular, time-consuming phone calls were turned into a source of revenue.

Marketing Materials:

✓ Sales Script
✓ Referral Program

Result! Realtor now makes $1,000 per day in addition to successful sales revenues with limited time investment.

Case Study No. 3

Personal Trainer

Business Type: Independent Contractor

Objective: Need to generate more new leads and create a loyal (more valuable) client base

Strategy: Risk Reversal and Service Packaging

Solution(s): The personal trainer needed to understand why first-time buyers are reluctant to purchase training services. In response, the first session was offered for free to clients who were qualified through a series of questions. This demonstrated credibility, empathy, insight, and most importantly the ability to provide a benefit to the person. Potential clients had the opportunity to evaluate the service before they opened their wallets.

Value Added Proposition: First session free, with package program of services available for $3,000 for Platinum clients.

Method: Advertise and promote free session

Marketing Materials:

✓ Training Program

✓ Sales Scripts

✓ Referral Program

Result! Personal Trainer tripled industry average revenues with this service package that sold for 10 times the industry average.

Case Study No. 4

Oil and Gas Company

Business Type: Large-format company

Objective: Need to find a way to keep customers coming back; most customers make 'one-time' purchases of large products that sell for approximately $70,000.

Strategy: Maintenance Program (Service Plan)

Solution(s): Machines sold for $70K and seldom had any issues inside five years. A warranty and Maintenance Program was developed to upsell each client, and provide an opportunity to 'get in the door' of the customer. A condition of the program is that we must come in quarterly to service the machine and ensure it was in good health.

Value Added Proposition: The $2,500 maintenance program was up-sold to each customer, providing an (almost) unconditional warranty and ease of mind.

Method: The serviceperson who made quarterly visits to each client also served as a salesperson that would look for other opportunities.

Marketing Materials:
- ✓ Collateral for other products
- ✓ Sales Script
- ✓ Questionnaire

Result! The 'lifetime value' of each client went up dramatically, and most sales were increased by $2,500 for the Maintenance Program.

Case Study No. 5

Accounting Company

Business Type: Service-based Company

Objective: Need to grow business and increase revenues.

Strategy: Education and Expertise Positioning

Solution(s): Educate the market regarding tax strategies 'The Government Didn't Want You to Know'. Position the business as the experts with cutting edge advice and innovative money saving solutions for clients.

Value Added Proposition: Potential clients were able to gain 'free' information from the business, without making a purchase, which eliminates the risk involved in finding an accountant.

Method: Accountant wrote educational and informative tax columns as well as developed a regular string of seminars.

Marketing Materials:

✓ Newspaper + Newsletter Columns

✓ Free Seminars

✓ Referral Program

Result! **Firmly established themselves as the 'go to' company for businesses wanting to pay less tax.**

Case Study No. 6

Music Teacher

Business Type: Independent Contractor

Objective: Need to generate more income to support ambitious business owner

Strategy: Risk Reversal + Education

Solution(s): Developed a free Loss Leader two-hour group lesson for adults. The most popular song requested was taught, and all participants were guaranteed to be able to play it after the two hours. His clients (adults) were not interested in playing technically well, just in knowing a few songs to play at Christmas, etc.

Value Added Proposition: Clients were not required to put down any money up front, and would have the opportunity to purchase a 12-month training course to continue to develop their skills.

Method: Loss Leader was heavily promoted, and at the end of the session the students were sold a 12-month training course (highly systemized and very little 'time' attached).

Marketing Materials:

✓ SWOT Analysis

✓ Advertisements

✓ Newsletter

✓ Joint Ventures

✓ Loss Leader

Result! Licensed the program. He reckons he will have made more money off 'Unchained Melody' than the Righteous Brothers!

Note: This music teacher had a solid back-end 12-month program to sell (very few piano teachers have anything that looks like this). Other teachers will/do have this available to them but will not be smart enough to capitalize on an opportunity to leverage someone else's program.

Case Study No. 7

Lawn Mowing Business

Business Type: Service-based Business

Objective: Find a way to increase revenues and reduce overhead.

Strategy: Competitor Research

Solution(s): Researched the five most successful businesses in their industry. Found the major competitors were companies selling 'licenses' rather than other lawn mowing companies. Created framework of everything needed to 'license'.

Value Added Proposition: Offer $30,000.00 licenses, rather than $50 lawn mowing jobs.

Method: Took everything the company was doing successfully to operate a 'lawn mowing business' and completed manuals for operations and marketing based on existing systems.

Marketing Materials:
- ✓ Operations Manual
- ✓ Marketing Manuals

Result! Licensed company and tripled previous year's sales with equal or reduced overhead.

PLUS: Realized everything that worked for the lawn mowing business could also work with minor changes for dog groomers and carpet cleaners. Also licensed these businesses.

Case Study No. 8

Community Supermarket

Business Type: Product-based Business

Issue: Needs to find a way to compete with other, larger, grocery stores and stop losing money.

Strategy: Joint Venture Marketing

Solution(s): Create a private label alternative with excellent branding and POS (point of sale) material. Joint venture with other small town supermarkets and ensured long-term strategy to 'compete with big boys'.

Value Added Proposition: Huge increases in profit margin for an excellent product

Method: Full-blown brand strategy.

Marketing Materials:

✓ Direct Mail

✓ Newspaper Ads

✓ Joint Ventures

Result! 22% increase in profitability.

Case Study No. 9

Local Restaurant

Business Type: Service-based Business

Issue: Revenues in a downward spiral.

Strategy: Target Market Research

Solution(s): Restaurant found that their clientele had changed, but they were still modeling their business on what had worked in the past. The name was changed from 'Family Restaurant' to 'Pastaria'; younger staff was recruited; a calendar of events was created to draw crowds; and the brand identity was updated. The new image was one that their desired clientele would resonate with.

Value Added Proposition: Past influential customers were invited to try the revamped restaurant for free (through gift certificates).

Method: Personal letters were mailed to all popular and influential people in the local area (athletes, successful business people, Mayor, Council Representatives, Newspaper publisher, etc.).

Marketing Materials:

✓ Personal Letters including Gift Certificates

✓ Calendar of Events

✓ New brand identity

Result! Revenues tripled over twelve months.

Case Study No. 10

Business Incubator

Business Type: Service-based Business

Objective: Increase occupancy in short-term offices and increase profit.

Strategy: Risk Reversal; Powerful Offer

Solution(s): A powerful offer was created and targeted at small to medium sized business owners currently operating from home. The offer included minimal financial investment, ease of transition, and no commitment.

Value Added Proposition: New clients were offered their first month free, no deposit, no contract, and a free moving service. There was no risk involved for the client, and a powerful business operation environment was provided.

Method: Direct mail sales letter to potential business clients who currently operate at home, with follow up calls made by contract salespeople to close the sales.

Marketing Materials:

✓ Sales Letter

✓ Sale Script

✓ Referral Program.

Result! Doubled profits in first year and sustained growth...

Case Study No. 11

Business Incubator

Business Type: Service-based Business

Objective: Business Incubator had developed a system that increased occupancy 22% above industry average (these basically doubled profits and needed to find new ways to grow the business.

Strategy: Purchase Competitors

Solution(s): Developed a list of competitors, and created a financial strategy to acquire them. Most of the business centers jumped at the chance to exit the business as they were operating at industry average. Grew business and market share immediately and also created a viable option for someone looking to sell.

Value Added Proposition: The clients received superior service and were provided with greater leverage through the expanded service centers.

Method: Direct mail piece to all business centers offering to purchase.

Marketing Materials:

✓ Sales Letter

✓ Sales Script

✓ Sales Presentation

Result! Bought several of their competitors, increased market share and brand awareness substantially, profits grew by 75%.

Case Study No. 12

Mortgage Broker

Business Type: Independent Contractor

Objective: Talented Mortgage Broker needs to grow clientele

Strategy: Expert Positioning

Solution(s): Increased her fees. Developed series of ongoing seminars, free information conferences, and wrote a column for magazines (hired ghost writer and licensed those available on the net).

Value Added Proposition: People wanted to work with her and seek her counsel because they were able to hear her opinions, numbers, success stories and advice prior to committing.

Method: Public speaking, free information nights and regular seminars/lunch and learns. Systemizing, recording and subsequently scripting initial consultations. She also leveraged existing joint venture with very popular real estate office.

Marketing Materials:
- ✓ Phone Script
- ✓ SWOT Analysis
- ✓ Fax Flyers
- ✓ Speakers Notes

Result! $27,245.00 profit in the first month as well as a successful business model that will be able to be licensed / sold.

Case Study No. 13

Hockey Rink (Australia)

Business Type: Service-based Business

Objective: Develop a school league for a sport that was not popular or well known in the Southern Hemisphere.

Strategy: Aggressive Education

Solution(s): Developed a skating program as lead generation and beginner hockey for those interested in trying the new sport. Becoming a school sport was difficult, but the clear and obvious route for immediate and sustainable growth.

Value Added Proposition: Kids and parents were offered an alternative sport activity, and the possibility of being an elite player in a new and emerging league.

Method: Created a school league driven from the ground up through the kids (they spoke to parents... who in turn spoke to the teachers) as opposed to the school system.

Marketing Materials:

✓ Fundraising Program (for local schools)

✓ Activities Program (skating, hockey, birthday parties, sleepovers)

✓ Referral Program (bring a friend)

Result! A school league with over 70 (paid) team's registered and state championships.

Case Study No. 14

Magician

Business Type: Independent Contractor

Objective: Make a profit!

Strategy: Value Added Packaging

Solution(s): A merchandise program was established to supplement the income generated from regular magic shows. Instead of relying on donations at the end of each show (like most street performers), a table was created with t-shirts and magic kits available for purchase. A salesperson was hired to man the table while the magician worked the crowd.

Value Added Proposition: Instead of a $5 donation, parents and kids could purchase $25 kits for home magic trick practice – a far better value.

Method: Table set up to sell magic kits and merchandise; salesperson was hired.

Marketing Materials:

✓ POS (point of sale) Material

✓ Magic Kits

✓ Uniforms + T-Shirts

✓ Referral Program

✓ Sales Training

Result! Tripled income immediately and was referred to larger paid gigs by audience members.

Case Study No. 15

Magazine Publisher

Business Type: Independent Contractor

Objective: Find a niche market used for publishing expertise. The successful magazine publisher sold her business with a 'non-compete' clause for a high profit. She wanted to continue working and this is the only business she knew.

Strategy: Education + Expert Positioning

Solution(s): Become a consultant. Train other struggling publishing businesses how to turn a handsome profit and avoid the common pitfalls of the business.

Value Added Proposition: Publishing businesses benefit from the expertise of a former competitor, without the high salary. The highly profit but high failure industry of publishing has access to a proven success.

Method: Sales letter followed by a phone call to all local publishing businesses.

Marketing Materials:
✓ Sales Script
✓ Referral Program
✓ Sales Letter

Result! She made more in this business than she did in the last!

Case Study No. 16

Carpet Cleaning Company

Business Type: Service-based Business

Objective: Need to increase repeat clients and reduce expense of attracting new clients.

Strategy: Client Education + Service Program

Solution(s): Most repeat clients only have their carpets cleaned every three to five years. A customer education program was created to encourage clients to increase that frequency to every six months. With hot extraction steam, the ongoing carpet cleaning program would provide health benefit for clients rather than a health detriment.

Value Added Proposition: The six-month frequency would provide clients with a health benefit, instead of a health detriment.

Method: Educate sales team and train all staff on new scripts, then create marketing material to back up claims.

Marketing Materials:
✓ Staff Sales Script
✓ Bonus Structure for Salespeople
✓ Marketing Collateral

Result! 27% (consistent with standard upselling statistics) of the clients bought into the program resulting in a HUGE increase in profitability.

So What Do You Do From Here?

The 3 Percent 'Winners Circle'™

I am confident this book is inspirational. However, inspiration without a decision and a decision without execution is futile. That's what the 97% do. They get what they have always gotten, because they continue to do what they have always not done.

If you execute the principles and strategies explained in this book, you will profitably grow your business. You will make your business the obvious choice for customers when it comes to buying what you sell.

Whenever you begin to shirk, re-read this book. Whenever you need to rekindle your inspiration, re-read this book. Every time you re-read this book, you will sustain your 'stick-to-itiveness' and determination to execute.

As a consultant, speaker, and coach, I help clients across the United States achieve success. My purpose in writing this book is to make a positive difference in your life.

Therefore, not being responsible for you, but responsible to you, I achieve my goal when you achieve yours. Look back on your life five years ago, and ask yourself...

'Do I want to be in this same place five years from now?'

Tired of so called experts and sales trainers telling you how to run your business when they've never done it themselves?

Ron Hequet – Driven by Results, Guided by Experience

I am one who has...**been there**...*owned / operated 8 business in 6 industries*...**done that**...consultant to client companies across the U.S. in over 20 industries...and **still doing it!**

Invest In Yourself and *Enroll today* in my **Private Mentor Program** for business owners and entrepreneurs that want to increase profits and begin to build cash surplus!

PMP™ partners with you both strategically (the 'what' of the future) and tactically (the 'how to' of today), to produce measurable results.

This exclusive program is perfect for you if...

✓ You have a burning desire to grow your business faster than ever before.
✓ You're sick and tired of struggling in trying to figure it out.

continue reading...

This program is NOT for you if...

- You'd rather struggle working hard, rather than right!
- You tend to be negative, whine, complain or blame outside circumstances for results.
- You'd rather stay right where you are, or
- You believe this program would be an **expense** instead of an **investment**.

The 3 Percent 'Winners Circle'™...find out if it's right for you by scheduling your free introductory assessment – go to...

www.RonHequet/Mentor-Programs.com

ADMISSION IS LIMITED: If there is no program availability at time of enrollment, you will be placed on the aged waiting list.

A Last Thought...

I would like you to help other business owner friends by giving a copy of this book to three people you care about. You in turn, will make a difference in their lives.

Order now by going to www.RonHequet.com or www.Amazon.com

Write down the three people to whom you will give a copy of this book:

1. _____

2. _____

3. _____

I appreciate the tribute you've given me by investing your valuable time and resources in this book.

Another Last Thought...

Next, I would like to really hear about all the successful ways you find to execute my proven strategies and tactics in your business or life. Please send me your results and breakthroughs.

I collect and study all of your achievement stories, largest to the smallest, financial or otherwise.

I want to receive your letters immediately after some of your first achievements. Tell me about your amazing results. Let me know how this book has shown you the way.

Please write to Ron Hequet, P.O. Box 2785, Weatherford, Texas 76086, or email to Ron@RonHequet.com

See you in the 3 Percent Winners Circle™

Additional Resources

BUILD YOUR COMPANY 180™
HOME OR OFFICE STEP BY STEP COURSE
THE ULTIMATE GUIDE FOR BUILDING PROFIT AND CASH IN ANY ECONOMY!

12 CD's, profit planning and cash flow spreadsheets and all the business planning fill-in forms you need, + over 6 hours of audio + action guide binder + bonus a CD and free bonus consultation with Ron Hequet

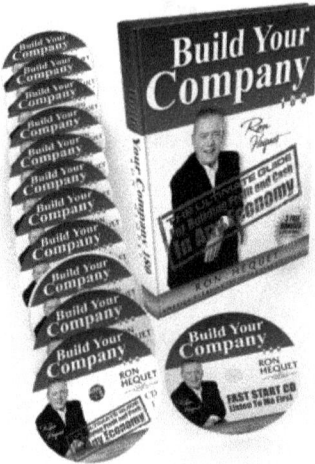

MINUTES MATTER©

GETTING MORE DONE IN LESS TIME

DVD, AUDIO CD AND ACTION GUIDE BOOK HOME STUDY COURSE

Time Management, Communication, Resolving Conflict and more...

To invest in additional resources...go to:
www.RonHequet.com

Additional Resources

CALL TO ORDER©

DISCOVER...HOW TO MEET LESS AND ACHIEVE MORE
DVD, AUDIO CD AND ACTION GUIDE BOOK
HOME STUDY COURSE

7 Faults you must avoid in order to meet for decisions, not information!
Learn the P.A.T. meeting system...take action / achieve more when you say...
'Call To Order'

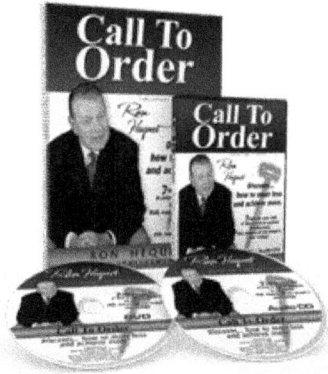

BUILD YOUR CAREER 180™

5 STREET SMART STRATEGIES TO NEVER
BY UNEMPLOYED OR UNDEREMPLOYED
IN ANY ECONOMY!

BOOK

Want Employment Security?
Learn How to Influence Profit and Cash
at Your Company

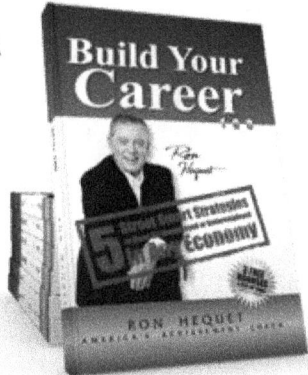

To invest in additional resources...go to:
www.RonHequet.com

Additional Resources

INVEST IN YOURSELF™
LEARN THE 'RIGHT' APPROACH, CONFIDENCE, TRAINING,
UPGRADE AND MOVEMENT!

DVD, AUDIO CD AND ACTION GUIDE BOOK
HOME STUDY COURSE

A special 'fast start' program...
don't work harder or smarter, but work 'right'!

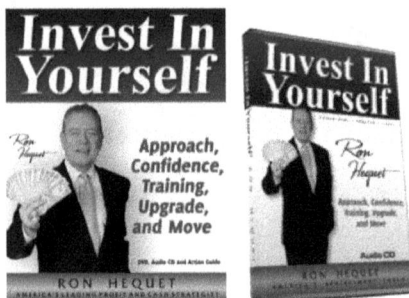

To invest in additional resources...go to:
www.RonHequet.com